God Likes Ants:
Every Week

God Likes Ants: Every Week

Fifty-two Scripture Reflections

Andrea M. Gilson

Foreword by Pastor Richard B. White

RESOURCE *Publications* • Eugene, Oregon

GOD LIKES ANTS: EVERY WEEK
Fifty-two Scripture Reflections

Copyright © 2013 Andrea M. Gilson. All rights reserved. Except for brief quotations in critical publications or reviews, no part of this book may be reproduced in any manner without prior written permission from the publisher. Write: Permissions, Wipf and Stock Publishers, 199 W. 8th Ave., Suite 3, Eugene, OR 97401.

Resource Publications
An Imprint of Wipf and Stock Publishers
199 W. 8th Ave., Suite 3
Eugene, OR 97401
www.wipfandstock.com

ISBN 13: 978-1-62564-103-8
Manufactured in the U.S.A.

For my father Bill

Contents

Foreword xi
Preface xiii
List of Abbreviations xv

Week 1—Proverbs 6:6 / 1

Week 2—Galatians 3:6–7 / 3

Week 3—Hebrews 13:2 / 5

Week 4—Proverbs 5:21 / 7

Week 5—Isaiah 28:9–10 / 9

Week 6—Mark 14:61–62 (Easter) / 11

Week 7—Luke 16:23–24 / 13

Week 8—1 Thessalonians 4:16–18 / 15

Week 9—John 9:31 / 17

Week 10—Luke 10:18 / 19

Week 11—Matthew 6:34 / 22

Week 12—Ecclesiastes 5:2 / 24

Week 13—Malachi 3:8 / 27

Contents

Week 14—John 5:14 / 30

Week 15—Colossians 2:14 / 32

Week 16—Luke 19:15 / 34

Week 17—Acts 17:22-23 / 36

Week 18—Philippians 2:14 / 38

Week 19—2 Corinthians 1:21-22 / 40

Week 20—Psalms 49:7 / 42

Week 21—Luke 12:25-26 / 45

Week 22—Revelation 2:17 / 47

Week 23—Proverbs 3:5-6 / 49

Week 24—Proverbs 14:12 / 51

Week 25—Romans 1:19-20 / 54

Week 26—Mark 7:6b-7 / 56

Week 27—Ecclesiastes 9:10a / 59

Week 28—Philippians 1:6 / 61

Week 29—Luke 24:39 / 63

Week 30—Zechariah 12:9 / 65

Week 31—Proverbs 27:1 / 68

Week 32—Hebrews 13:16 / 70

Week 33—Isaiah 65:24 / 72

Week 34—Psalms 118:18 / 74

Contents

Week 35—2 Corinthians 11:3 / 76

Week 36—Job 19:25-26 / 79

Week 37—Ephesians 5:20 (Thanksgiving) / 81

Week 38—2 Thessalonians 3:6 / 83

Week 39—Matthew 4:4 / 85

Week 40—Psalms 91:11-12 / 87

Week 41—Isaiah 9:6-7 (Christmas) / 90

Week 42—2 Timothy 2:23 / 92

Week 43—Matthew 10:34 / 94

Week 44—Matthew 18:21-22 / 96

Week 45—James 5:16 / 98

Week 46—Mark 10:27 / 100

Week 47—2 Corinthians 4:8-9 / 102

Week 48—Psalms 122:6 / 104

Week 49—Proverbs 12:16 / 106

Week 50—Zechariah 14:12 / 108

Week 51—Proverbs 24:17-18 / 110

Week 52—1 Timothy 1:17 / 112

Appendix A—What I believe / 115

Foreword

ANDREA HAS A UNIQUE and insightful understanding of daily experiences. She sees the purpose in the mundane and seemingly insignificant experiences of life. Her thoughts and insights stimulate meditation and her questions draw one to the scripture for answers. I always enjoy reading her writing and it is always both a challenge to my personal walk and an inspiration to follow Christ.

It was my joy to be her pastor and worshipping friend for several years. I pray that all who read her writing will be as blessed as I have. It is my prayer that God will encourage and challenge those who read this book to follow Him by reading and understanding the writer's purpose.

Pastor Richard B. White—May 7, 2013

Preface

The conception of *God Likes Ants* was on January 7, 2011. It was just a couple of months later when the Lord inspired me to begin. Seated on my bed in a shared room I rented while transitioning to my new home in Oregon, I very suddenly knew it was time for my idea to be born. Some things you just know God is leading.

I wanted to write. God wanted me to write about him. The intention was to put on paper my thoughts about his Word using individual Bible verses. Proverb 6:6 became my starting point. "Go to the ant, thou sluggard; consider her ways and be wise." I heeded that advice and my laziness was ended, in regards to getting started on this project anyway. The line by Solomon taught me that God likes ants and according to this verse, it is because they are go-getters.

The writing got done every Thursday night henceforth and my friends and family received my perspectives in their e-mail. They encouraged me and I learned that more people in my life loved the Lord than I knew. It was further inspiration to continue. One advised that making a compilation of my "editions" would be a blessing to me and others. I agreed and that idea remained in the back of my mind until this book came together.

Written in the manner of a column, all perspectives and interpretations in *God Likes Ants: Every Week* are my opinions. I ask my readers to remember this as they read.

Preface

As a lay Christian, I spent decades in Bible study and discussions which led to these writings.

I follow no particular religion but trust in God's Word for direction. I consider myself a "generic" Christian with no labels other than a person that loves and trusts in God in three persons and believes scripture is inspired by the Almighty above.

The reflections in *God Likes Ants: Every Week* differ in length and complexity. My hope is that new and mature Christians will find milk and meat in the pages. I further hope to attract skeptics of Christ to become interested in Bible study and learn acceptance.

There are weeks dedicated to Christmas, Easter, and Thanksgiving. I have noted these in the Table of Contents since readers will begin the book in whatever week they wish. It would be awkward for a discussion about Easter to be read in August unless the reader was informed. I began writing in March originally so the holidays fall in that pattern. I use personal anecdotes and supporting scripture in my writing. Sometimes, I try my hand at humor. Bear with me.

The Authorized King James Version of the Bible is my trusted translation and all verses used are thus taken. It is a pleasure to enjoy the old style of using language. Please use this little book for personal Bible study and to share in small groups to invoke discussion. I hope my book will edify and develop your relationship to Jesus, our Lord. Enjoy.

Andrea M. Gilson—May 16, 2013

List of Abbreviations

Genesis—Gen

Exodus—Exod

Leviticus—Lev

Numbers—Num

Deuteronomy—Deut

Joshua—Josh

Judges—Judg

Ruth—Ruth

Samuel—Sam

Kings—Kgs

Chronicles—Chr

Ezra—Ezra

Nehemiah—Neh

Esther—Esth

Job—Job

Psalms—Ps (pl. Pss)

Proverbs—Prov

Ecclesiastes—Eccl

Song of Solomon—Song

Isaiah—Isa

List of Abbreviations

Jeremiah—Jer

Lamentations—Lam

Ezekiel—Ezek

Daniel—Dan

Hosea—Hos

Joel—Joel

Amos—Amos

Obadiah—Obad

Jonah—Jonah

Micah—Mic

Nahum—Nah

Habakkuk—Hab

Zephaniah—Zeph

Haggai—Hag

Zechariah—Zech

Malachi—Mal

Matthew—Matt

Mark—Mark

Luke—Luke

John—John

Acts—Acts

Romans—Rom

Corinthians—Cor

Galatians—Gal

Ephesians—Eph

Philippians—Phil

List of Abbreviations

Colossians—Col

Thessalonians—Thess

Timothy—Tim

Titus—Titus

Philemon—Phlm

Hebrews—Heb

James—Jas

Peter—Pet

John—John

Jude—Jude

Revelation—Rev

Week 1

Scripture text—Proverbs 6:6

Go to the ant, thou sluggard; consider her ways and be wise.

I chose the above text for the inaugural impression of *God Likes Ants: Every Week*. It will be the identifying verse for this publication. This small verse teaches us humans much about what God considers wise behavior. Ants are small. They work together for common good and generally go unnoticed.

There are many species of ants. I do not think that God expects us to become scientific experts on the diverse personality traits of each type of ant but to take the common knowledge we have of them and apply it to our lives. I quickly think of diligent, focused, meek, and determined as adjectives for the little critters.

A strong point that comes to my mind is how they concentrate on the task they are working on. They do not get distracted from their job. They lift heavy weights compared to their size and maneuver over untold obstacles to accomplish their mission.

They work together to satisfy common goals. I love to watch ants and I urge anyone to take a few minutes next time you spy them to watch them closely. We can learn

God Likes Ants: Every Week

many lessons from God's creation; the ant is a tiny example. Work hard, work together, and remain on task.

Week 2

Scripture text—Galatians 3:6-7

Even as Abraham believed God, and it was accounted to him for righteousness. Know ye therefore that they which are of faith, the same are the children of Abraham.

THE OLD TESTAMENT IS not just the teaching of the Jewish law. It is a program of learning about faith. Some try to separate out the New Testament as being about faith and the Old Testament to be cast aside as antiquated and not pertinent to the rest of us (Gentiles). It may be antiquated but it surely is pertinent.

Scripture is clear that for those of us that put our faith in God we are also of the chosen. It cannot be denied, that the children of Abraham, *Isaac, and Jacob* were chosen to be his special people. Christians that accept God's plan of redemption are adopted into the Jewish family. This is why I feel proud when I wear my Jewish Star of David. I am now a spiritual Jew through my faith in Christ, adopted into God's family.

The purpose of the law is to prove that we cannot attain God's favor through efforts of our own. It is impossible. Faith is the key. Many Old Testament examples come to mind besides Abraham—how about Noah. He built that boat and gathered those animals while his neighbors ridiculed him. That's faith. The New Testament book of Hebrews is a great place for compact review of Old Testament saints that came to God and believed through faith. Without faith it is impossible to please God (Heb 11:6). Ask him to build your faith today.

Week 3

Scripture text—Hebrews 13:2

Be not forgetful to entertain strangers: for thereby some have entertained angels unawares.

THIS VERSE REMINDS US to be kind to everyone we encounter. God can send his messengers to interact with us humans in any way he chooses. This reality should make us consider the words we use, the way out body language speaks, and whether or not we love others as ourselves—which he commands. It is hard to do that indeed. All people fail to meet God's holy standard. I miss the mark daily.

God commands us to love those that love us and those that hate us. It is no sacrifice for us to love a person who loves us, that's simple (Matt 5:46–47). We should strive to always treat people well. The person at the bus stop today may be a heavenly creature in disguise.

It is a blessing to know that the angels are here to serve as our ministers (Heb 1:14). They were created to serve God. They caution humans several places in scripture not to worship them but God alone. Knowing that they are all around us going about our Father's business is a tremendous reality. Likewise, Satan's spiritual followers are here too. We must learn discernment through prayer and scripture study. The unseen world is real. More so than what we humans can comprehend.

Just to be on the safe side and keep God smiling down on you, consider that those around you could be on a mission from above. Don't disappoint God and mistreat his servants.

Week 4

Scripture text—Proverbs 5:21

For the ways of man are before the eyes of the LORD,
and he pondereth all his goings.

How exciting to know that the Creator is interested in all of our goings. We can rest assured that we are never alone. It is convicting to consider our actions when we remember with each moment that he is pondering our activities. Think about when we ponder something. It means to weigh in the mind, to deliberate. Our Lord cares enough about us to spend time thinking about our lives. He did not create people just to forget about them. He wants to know us inside and out. He certainly does anyway but he prefers if it is a mutual attraction. He considers our hearts and our minds. He is our strength and our purpose.

I want to claim the promise he makes in 2 Chronicles 16:9a, "For the eyes of the LORD run to and fro throughout the whole earth, to shew himself strong in the behalf of them whose heart is perfect toward him."

So many Bible verses lead to this truth. I pray like David did for God to clean my heart and renew my spirit (Ps 51:10). The great king prayed in this manner after his sin with Bathsheba. No matter what you have done, rejoice that God ponders your heart. Stay in touch with him all through the day. He is thinking about you and waiting for your prayer.

Week 5

Scripture text—Isaiah 28:9-10

Whom shall he teach knowledge? and whom shall he make to understand doctrine? them that are weaned from the milk, and drawn from the breasts. For precept must be upon precept, precept upon precept; line upon line, line upon line; here a little, and there a little.

SCRIPTURE CAN BE CONFUSING. It takes much study to put it all together. God knows this truth. He uses milk and meat allegorically to represent scriptural depth. Like newborn babies that consume milk from the mother's breast, people that are new to Bible study must have patience and try not to digest the hard stuff too quickly. This will build confusion and the untruth that scripture contradicts itself and is not literal.

Scripture builds upon itself like Isaiah the prophet states. It explains itself when studied diligently. Indeed it is difficult even for those that have studied a long time. Take the time to understand the basics before biting off more than you can chew. Meat takes much chewing. Beginners are wise to remain in the Gospel of John and the book of Romans at first. All the basics are there, and then branch out. Always ask for God's help in understanding his truths.

God Likes Ants: Every Week

There are no contradictions in the Bible and it is literal. God does use analogies, metaphors, and parables but he is sure to let the reader know exactly when he is doing that. Otherwise, he means exactly what he says. I find Ezekiel especially challenging. If new Christians open to Judges chapter 19, they may slam the Bible closed and run from it.

Paul said in 1 Corinthians 3:2, "I have fed you with milk, and not with meat: for hitherto ye were not able to bear it, neither yet now are ye able." God says that we will find him when we seek him with all our heart. It is a good thing that understanding the entire Bible is not a condition of salvation. Believing in and accepting God's gift of his son, Jesus, to atone for our sins is the ticket. You will surely want to spend time daily studying the scriptures, old and new. He gave us the Bible for the purpose of knowing him and his will. Dig in and be fed; nothing else really matters.

Week 6

Scripture text—Mark 14:61–62

But he held his peace, and answered nothing. Again the high priest asked him, and said unto him, Art thou the Christ, the Son of the Blessed? And Jesus said, I am: and ye shall see the Son of man sitting on the right hand of power, and coming in the clouds of heaven.

Easter week is the most important few days in all of history, the basis for Christianity. Thirty-three years after being born humbly in a barn in Bethlehem, our Savior completed his mission to take the sins of humankind onto himself. After three days, God brought him back to life from the grave to become the first fruit of the resurrection. Now those of us who believe and trust in him will live forever, and not just in spirit. Christ invited his disciples to touch his body afterwards to see and believe it was flesh. We will receive new bodies as well, incorruptible, immortal bodies in which to enjoy eternity with him. First Corinthians 15:54 says, "So when this corruptible shall have put on incorruption, and this mortal shall have put on immortality, then shall be brought to pass the saying that is written, Death is swallowed up in victory."

God Likes Ants: Every Week

The first time Christ came to earth was in humility to give the New Covenant. He is returning again. When he does it will be in great power and majesty. All will see him and most will mourn because of him since they have not believed in him. Hebrews 10:31 says, "It is a fearful thing to fall into the hands of the living God."

If you do not know Christ, the Easter season is a perfect time to learn about him and invite him to govern your life. Find a Bible faithful church near you. Read the Gospels—Matthew, Mark, Luke, and John. At that first Good Friday he went to his death quietly like a lamb to a slaughter. He knew he must obey his mission and suffer the curse of crucifixion so that we can claim his blood as the covering for our sins when God asks why we are worthy of Heaven. In ourselves we surely are not. His death is God's unimaginable gift to each of us. Please accept it.

Week 7

Scripture text—Luke 16:23-24

And in hell he lift up his eyes, being in torments, and seeing Abraham afar off, and Lazarus in his bosom. And he cried and said, Father Abraham, have mercy on me, and send Lazarus, that he may dip the tip of his finger in water, and cool my tongue; for I am in torment in this flame.

JESUS TALKED MUCH ABOUT Hell. It is a real place that God created as punishment for Satan and the angels that rebelled with him (Matt 25:41, Rev 12:9). It will be a hot place where people that fail to recognize Jesus as Lord will spend eternity.

In the final chapter everyone will get bodily resurrected and face God's judgment. Hopefully you will have the blood of Christ to atone for your failings so he will allow you into his blessed presence. Have faith in his blood to save you.

The story in Luke 16 should be studied in its entirety from 19-31 to get the full gist of the story. The point is that the rich during their lives often do not recognize a need for God while the poor more often cry out to the living God. Worship of material items and prestige push God aside. "And again I say unto you, It is easier for a camel to go through the eye of a needle, than for a rich man to enter into the kingdom of God" (Matt 19:24, Mark 10:25).

The story also shows that upon death our fate is settled. The rich man went immediately into the flame and Lazarus, the poor beggar, was with Abraham enjoying Heaven. The rich man's plea for a drop of water was denied. The chasm between Heaven and Hell is fixed. He also asked for his living brothers to receive a visit from Lazarus's ghost to warn them. This request was denied as well. Abraham reminded the condemned man that the word of God has already warned them. There are other places in scripture where God reminds humankind that nature itself declares God loudly to the creatures of the earth (Ps 19:1, Rom 1:19–20). Get on the winning side.

Week 8

Scripture text—1 Thessalonians 4:16–18

For the Lord himself shall descend from heaven with a shout, with the voice of the archangel, and with the trump of God: and the dead in Christ shall rise first: Then we which are alive and remain shall be caught up together with them in the clouds, to meet the Lord in the air: and so shall we ever be with the Lord. Wherefore comfort one another with these words.

These words refer to the rapture (transport) of the church of Christ. I wanted to write this so that if one day suddenly millions of people are missing from the earth, those left behind will know that the event has been predicted in the Bible. The explanations that will surface after the event will be false.

All prophesies in the Bible come to pass. We can know with confidence that God will complete the plan he outlined in his Word. Many books have been written on this topic. Study Bible prophesies to know. What a pleasure to learn that God has given us our history in advance.

Rapture is a man-made name given to the event of transportation described in many places throughout scripture. A few places to study are Matthew 24, 1 Corinthians 15:51–52, and 1 Thessalonians 4:13–18. Transport is the clear message. Throughout human history two people have been transported in this way without facing physical death. Enoch and Elijah were favored by God and taken by him directly, the way Christians can expect to be taken before God's wrath is unleashed on our planet. Learn about Enoch in Genesis 5:24 and Elijah in 2 Kings 2:1-11.

In story after story in the Bible, God's own are removed prior to his wrath. It is not a fantasy of escapism but God's modus operandi. The kingdom of God will be played out as he told us. Jesus will be the ruler on earth as he is in Heaven. Do we not pray this in the Lord's Prayer practically without thinking about the meaning of the words?

It will be such a blessing to be among his before the rapture. It will be terrible for those who decide for Christ afterwards during the time of the great tribulation. It is all available to know. The Bible can be confusing. If you have trouble, use a prophecy guide that will point you to the places to study in the Word.

Do not wonder. Know that you can count yourself worthy to escape the wrath to come. Trust in Christ for your life.

Week 9

Scripture text—John 9:31

Now we know that God heareth not sinners: but if any man be a worshipper of God, and doeth his will, him he heareth.

This may be a hard truth for some to swallow but until a person has been cleansed by the blood of Christ, he/she cannot enter into God's presence with prayer. Only Christians can expect access to God in prayer because in his eyes we are no longer sinners but saints. The penalty that belongs to us (death—Rom 6:23) has been laid on Jesus Christ so that those who believe that truth may appear sinless before God.

God knows the state of each heart. He will measure our true devotion. His ear is open to his own. In Matthew 6:7, Jesus was speaking and he said that many that pray do so out of habit not having any intimate relationship with him. He calls their prayers vain repetitions and he refers to the people praying as heathens. They should save the effort. God is not listening. Find the perfect antidote to your sin problem (gift of the cross) and then enter the throne room freely. Those of us who know and follow Christ are not heathens but heirs to the throne of God with Christ our Savior (Rom 8:14–17).

God Likes Ants: Every Week

It is discouraging to know that so many people pray to a God that is unknown to them. They wonder why their prayers are not answered and their lives do not improve. Time and again, folks plead their case with a vague spirit in the sky and do not study the Bible to find out who he is or what he wants from us. The feature verse of the week describes it. He wants worship and obedience. He will hear you if you trust in his plan of salvation and appreciate his astonishing gift. "The gift of God is eternal life through Jesus Christ our Lord" (Rom 6:23b). Consider the grim truth in Matthew 7:21–23:

> Not everyone that saith unto me, Lord, Lord, shall enter into the kingdom of heaven; but he that doeth the will of my Father which is in heaven. Many will say to me in that day, Lord, Lord, have we not prophesied in thy name? and in thy name have cast out devils? and in thy name done many wonderful works? And then will I profess unto them, I never knew you: depart from me, ye that work iniquity.

Trust in Jesus Christ. Get to know him through scripture study and prayer. Then know that you are heard since you are a member of his family. Even better news for those that are born again (by the Spirit—John 3:3–6), we have the help of the Holy Spirit making up for our failings and confusion. "Likewise the Spirit also helpeth our infirmities: for we know not what we should pray for as we ought: but the Spirit itself maketh intercession for us with groanings which cannot be uttered" (Rom 8:26). That is a heavy promise and a peace bringing truth.

Week 10

Scripture text—Luke 10:18

And he said unto them, I beheld Satan as lightning fall from heaven.

WHAT A GREAT REMINDER that our Lord is eternal as the Holy Trinity. Theologians disagree about the time of Lucifer's rebellion and his casting out of Heaven. Some believe it was before Adam and Eve and some a time afterward. Nonetheless, Jesus Christ was certainly present in Heaven at the time.

It is important to know that Jesus was not only born as a child in Bethlehem in a manger to atone for our sins with his death some thirty-three years later, but that he could only do that because he was sinless and perfect. He was God incarnate. What a sacrifice he made for us. He came to live on this planet with his creatures for a time and was exposed to the same situations that are common to all people, yet he remained true to his mission to redeem us and overcome Satan for good.

When Christ uttered "It is finished" (John 19:30b), he meant that his death conquered Death. His mission was accomplished. Happy is any person that believes this truth.

Since Lucifer (renamed Satan) was cast like lightning from Heaven, he has been making use of his time accusing God's saints and hoping to gain a populace to join him in Hell.

God Likes Ants: Every Week

Consider Job 2:1–2, "Again there was a day when the sons of God came to present themselves before the LORD, and Satan came also among them to present himself before the LORD. And the LORD said unto Satan, From whence comest thou? And Satan answered the LORD, and said, From going to and fro in the earth, and from walking up and down in it." Peter similarly said in 1 Peter 5:8, "Be sober, be vigilant; because your adversary the devil, as a roaring lion, walketh about, seeking whom he may devour."

Those of us who are Christians are indwelt with the Holy Spirit. Satan is limited in what he can do to us, yet he works hard to make us grieve the Spirit within us. Unbelievers have no such protection and are wide open to Satan's influence. Until the very end of time, we will have to contend with the prideful angel of former splendor (Isa 14:12–15). The spirit world is real. It is necessary to wear the whole armor of God to stand against the wiles of the devil. The enemy is exposed and the tools God supplies for protection are told us in Ephesians 6:12–18:

> For we wrestle not against flesh and blood, but against principalities, against powers, against the rulers of the darkness of this world, against spiritual wickedness in high places. Wherefore take unto you the whole armour of God, that ye may be able to withstand in the evil day, and having done all, to stand. Stand therefore, having your loins girt about with truth, and having on the breastplate of righteousness; And your feet shod with the preparation of the gospel of peace; Above all, taking the shield of faith, wherewith ye shall be able to quench all the fiery darts of the wicked. And take the helmet of salvation, and the sword of the Spirit, which is the word of God: Praying always with all prayer and supplication in the Spirit, and watching thereunto with all perseverance and supplication for all saints.

Week 10

Often people want to make themselves into more than they are, which is created beings. It is too late for the rebellious angels. They cannot be redeemed. Humans are special in that sense. The commonly used phrase *pride cometh before a fall* is Biblically based (Prov 16:18). Satan fell fast. At the final judgment, Satan will be cast into Hell for good (Rev 20). A third of angels and the wide road of humans will have to join him. Ask Jesus to rescue you from that terrible fate.

Our God is eternal as God the Father, God the Son (Jesus Christ—the Word), and God the Holy Ghost (1 John 5:7). Jesus is in Heaven now and was in the beginning.

Week 11

Scripture text—Matthew 6:34

Take therefore no thought for the morrow:
for the morrow shall take thought for the things of itself.
Sufficient unto the day is the evil thereof.

It is one of the hardest things to relax and let God do his thing in our lives. We tend to lay awake at night wondering about the project at work, how we will pay the month's bills, our children, and even the smallest concerns like which shoes to buy.

Scripture reminds us that instead we are to rest in his provision. He knows what we need before we ask him (Matt 6:8). Worry is a sin since it shows lack of faith. God says if you have only the faith as a mustard seed you can move mountains (Matt 17:20). Imagine if you had faith the size of an avocado pit. He is aware of everything including our baseless worries and our struggles with faith.

We serve an omnipotent, sovereign God and we are his children. Remember how well your earthly father works to please you and meet your needs (mine is a great example of this). More so your heavenly Father who is above all and limitlessly capable knows your needs and wants (Luke 11:13). He desires to be a part of each detail of your life.

Week 11

Let him. He has even the hairs on your head counted. He knows the name of every star. He is aware when one of his birds falls from the sky.

He can surely meet all of his children's needs. The trouble is sometimes we feel like what we want is not what we get from God. In this case, again, trust and have faith in him who is faithful. Like any good father he has our best interests at heart, and he is high enough above any of our situations to survey the entire issue. He gives us what is best and if we follow his guidance we are sure to be happier because of it. Take things one day at a time.

As the verse says, sufficient for the day is the trouble for the day without thinking about the potentials of tomorrow. We face daily evils as we fight against the powers of the air, spirits that try to vex us and steal our tranquility (Eph 6:12). In addition to that, God gives us things to do for the day in just the right dose for the day. He does not want his children to live in constant worry. He gives us things to handle in manageable doses and we are to trust him for the rest.

"But seek ye first the kingdom of God, and his righteousness; and all these things shall be added unto you" (Matt 6:33). Let go and let God—really, he wants to.

Week 12

Scripture text—Ecclesiastes 5:2

Be not rash with thy mouth, and let not thine heart be hasty
to utter any thing before God: for God is in heaven,
and thou upon earth: therefore let thy words be few.

When wondering about this topic, I thought about how hard it is to hold one's tongue when suddenly angry or hurt. It seems that if cussing has been any part of a person's past, the words remain near the surface waiting to vex the Spirit. It does not help that Satan, our enemy, wants us to insult our Lord and others with bad language at every turn.

I do not mean to limit this discussion to cuss words alone. Words that are not thought through or that do not edify the hearer can be rash. Silence really is golden. There is a saying that you can keep your mouth closed and let people wonder if you are a fool or you can speak and secure the matter. I do not know if that adage has Biblical origins but scripture has endless similar advice. I suspect that the tongue can only be tamed through prayer and practice. In fact, God tells us in James 3:8, "But the tongue can no man tame; it is an unruly evil, full of deadly poison."

The Bible describes the foul workings of the tongue and those that allow it: wicked doer (my favorite—even better than evil doer), liar, fool, vain, deceitful, violent, treacherous, a sepulcher, poison, iniquity, guile, and arrogant.

Sinning with one's words is an overlooked ill that society tends to accept as harmless. All sin is an affront to the Creator. In 1 Samuel 2:3, he says, "Talk no more so exceeding proudly; let not arrogancy come out of your mouth: for the LORD is a God of knowledge, and by him actions are weighed." Speaking is surely an action. God will pay attention and hold us responsible whether with eternal judgment for non-believers or through chastisement during our earthy lives for his saints.

Abuse of language is not natural as a matter of fact. Consider, "And the tongue is a fire, a world of iniquity: so is the tongue among our members, that it defileth the whole body, and setteth on fire the course of nature; and it is set on fire of hell" (Jas 3:6). Indeed, much attention is paid to the problems with things that we put into our mouths (alcohol, drugs, tobacco, coffee, sugar, fat) and they are worth consideration. Do not ignore what the Bible says though, "Not that which goeth into the mouth defileth a man; but that which cometh out of the mouth, this defileth a man" (Matt 15:11).

God takes this seriously. What can be done? Pray and practice. God promises that he will be our present help in trouble. Do what the feature verse says; be not rash with thy mouth. Practice silence. For the other times, if you must speak, consult the Lord. In the Psalms and Proverbs examples of the Lord's help with the mouth are countless. Also, study these verses: Exodus 4:12, "Now therefore go, and I will be with thy mouth, and teach thee what thou shalt say" and Numbers 23:12, "And he answered and said, Must I not take heed to speak that which the LORD hath put in my mouth?"

God Likes Ants: Every Week

Make your prayer, "Set a watch, O LORD, before my mouth; keep the door of my lips" (Ps 141:3). Keep God utmost in your conscious and remain in ceaseless communion with him. He will guide your words if you ask him to and will convict you of wrong doings. "Whoso keepeth his mouth and his tongue keepeth his soul from troubles" (Prov 21:23). Just be nice, and quiet.

Week 13

Scripture text—Malachi 3:8

Will a man rob God? Yet ye have robbed me.
But ye say, Wherein have we robbed thee?
In tithes and offerings.

People work hard for their money. Often their habit is to cling to their increase like a life raft. Even so, it is important to remember that everything on this planet and in the universe belongs to God. "For by him were all things created, that are in heaven, and that are in earth, visible and invisible, whether they be thrones, or dominions, or principalities, or powers: all things were created by him, and for him" (Col 1:16).

God promises to take care of us. It is our duty to trust in him. "The just shall live by faith" (Hab 2:4b, Rom 1:17b, Gal 3:11b, and Heb 10:38a). Students of scripture will find that God tends to repeat the most important truths. The Lord is the only life raft we need.

He asks us to, "Honour the LORD with thy substance, and with the firstfruits of all thine increase" (Prov 3:9). This is a command statement. If we are to expect blessings from our God we are to give back a portion of what he has freely given us to benefit his kingdom. Even the patriarch Abraham gave a tenth of his spoils (Heb 7:4).

The ideal way to tithe (give the first tenth of all increase) is as a contribution to your church family. If you are not involved in a particular church then give regular donations to a God purposeful charity. If it is all you can do, give the 10 percent to homeless people on the street. This last is a choice as spoken of in Deuteronomy 26:12. The Lord sees you; he will bless you.

Do not; however, loudly proclaim your godliness since you are tithing (and this is true for fasting as well). Your boasting may cancel out your tithing. Consider Matthew's words in 6:1–4:

> Take heed that ye do not your alms before men, to be seen of them: otherwise ye have no reward of your Father which is in heaven. Therefore when thou doest thine alms, do not sound a trumpet before thee, as the hypocrites do in the synagogues and in the streets, that they may have glory of men. Verily I say unto you, they have their reward. But when thou doest alms, let not thy left hand know what thy right hand doeth: That thine alms may be in secret: and thy Father which seeth in secret himself shall reward thee openly.

Make it a habit to determine what a tenth of your increase is and obey God by putting it to his use. He does not need your money but he wants your devotion and obedience. It will not be a hardship. God is faithful. He tells us in Malachi that if we are not faithful to this requirement then we are robbing him and will be cursed. He allows, even asks us in Malachi 3:10b to challenge him about the benefit of tithing. "Prove me now herewith, saith the LORD of hosts, if I will not open you the windows of heaven, and pour you

Week 13

out a blessing, that there shall not be room enough to receive it."

The Bible has much to say about money in a variety of applications. The most famous may be, "No man can serve two masters: for either he will hate the one, and love the other; or else he will hold to the one, and despise the other. Ye cannot serve God and mammon" (Matt 6:24 and Luke 16:13). Again God chooses to repeat himself. Mammon means wealth/riches. All things are given to us by God. Make it a practice to share with him what is already his.

Week 14

Scripture text—John 5:14

Afterward Jesus findeth him in the temple, and said unto him, Behold, thou art made whole: sin no more, lest a worse thing come unto thee.

Jesus performed many miracles and after healing a man's lameness he gave the happy man the above caveat. God chooses us for redemption and works to make our lives more and more like his Son. Christ was the only sinless human to ever live (remember that Jesus was fully man while remaining fully God). While we cannot acquire perfection as long as we are hostage to our flesh, we are to give it our best effort.

Those who are sealed with the blood of Christ need not fear eternal damnation but would be wise to fear the Lord's chastisement. The lives we are living here and now are in the hands of the living God. He directs all of our circumstances. It is best to remain in his favor. If you are a Christian that does not walk in God's path, you will certainly notice your life stressing you out at some point. God works in his own special time frame that we cannot understand. But rest assured, he will correct you. Proverbs 3:12

says, "For whom the LORD loveth he correcteth; even as a father the son in whom he delighteth."

He advocates harsh punishment as anyone that is familiar with the Bible knows. Also, he recommends that loving human parents punish their children for their own good. It is the parent's job to set the child on the right path. "He that spareth his rod hateth his son: but he that loveth him chasteneth him betimes" (Prov 13:24). God is the best parent. He knows how to contend with each of us in his own way and time.

He is serious about sin. It must be recognized and shunned. "Be not deceived; God is not mocked: for whatsoever a man soweth, that shall he also reap" (Gal 6:7). The difference between godly and ungodly behavior is not hard to discern with the help of the Holy Spirit. Just to be certain, he gives us a list in Galatians 5:19–23:

> Now the works of the flesh are manifest, which are these; Adultery, fornication, uncleanness, lasciviousness, idolatry, witchcraft, hatred, variance, emulations, wrath, strife, seditions, heresies, envyings, murders, drunkenness, revellings, and such like: of the which I tell you before, as I have also told you in time past, that they which do such things shall not inherit the kingdom of God. But the fruit of the Spirit is love, joy, peace, longsuffering, gentleness, goodness, faith, meekness, temperance: against such there is no law.

Was the man in the story in John lame because of his sin? or his parents sin? or no sin at all? Only God knows the answer. He is a mighty sovereign God and he does whatever he chooses. His warning shows that our actions do come with consequences. Why take a chance with God's fancy. Listen for his voice, meditate on his word for guidance, and pray for wisdom. Then, go and sin no more.

Week 15

Scripture text—Colossians 2:14

Blotting out the handwriting of ordinances that was against us, which was contrary to us, and took it out of the way, nailing it to his cross.

THE ABOVE VERSE BRINGS to mind God with a file dedicated to each of our lives. We know he keeps track of our uprising and our down sitting (Ps 139:2). We also know that he is fond of the written word. I like the idea of a big bottle of white-out that he uses to make our transgressions disappear.

Once we accept Christ into our lives, the Holy Spirit indwells us convicting us of our actions. We are set free from slavery to sin and can rest assured that from then on our slate is clean with God as far as our assured salvation is concerned. Christ is our intercessor. Instead of God seeing our sins, he sees the blood of his Son. Romans 8:1 says, "There is therefore now no condemnation to them which are in Christ Jesus, who walk not after the flesh, but after the Spirit."

What a gift. We must be careful not to take his generosity for granted in the guise of Christian liberty (Rom 6:1). That is not grateful. Indeed, our works will be brought to

Week 15

bear on us as believers in regards to the rewards God gives us in Heaven.

Writing to fellow believers, Paul reminds the Corinthians, "For we must all appear before the judgment seat of Christ; that every one may receive the things done in his body, according to that he hath done, whether it be good or bad" (2 Cor 5:10). This is called the Bema Judgment in some explanations. There is no punishment in Heaven for Christians; only rewards given for the positive works accomplished. Why not do as much good as possible?

In 1 Corinthians 3:13–15, Paul tells us, "Every man's work shall be made manifest: for the day shall declare it, because it shall be revealed by fire; and the fire shall try every man's work of what sort it is. If any man's work abide which he hath built thereupon, he shall receive a reward. If any man's work shall be burned, he shall suffer loss: but he himself shall be saved; yet so as by fire."

The believer's sins are removed from barring access to the throne for prayer and communion with God. Knowing Christ makes that possible. What we do with the gift of Christ and how we live determines our degree of joyfulness or regret upon facing our Savior. I hope to have some good things piled up after the lot is passed through the fire. He gives us an incentive to do good works.

God keeps track of the sins of unbelievers and their sin remains. In the end, unless they accept the gift and claim the blood of Christ, they are bound for everlasting fire. I am so happy that my name will be found in the Book of Life (Rev 21:27). Will yours? Ask him to write it in there now and become intimate with him. Seek and ye shall find.

Week 16

Scripture text—Luke 19:15

And it came to pass, that when he was returned, having received the kingdom, then he commanded these servants to be called unto him, to whom he had given the money, that he might know how much every man had gained by trading.

In this story, the nobleman gave money to his servants to care for while he went out to secure a kingdom. Upon his return, he meant to get his property (his money and more) back. He praised the first for doubling his money through wise investing. Likewise a second servant made a profit on the amount entrusted to him. The third; however, fearing his lord's station, simply kept his ten pounds in a safe place to return when required.

This lack of proper stewardship of the money angered the nobleman. He rewarded the first two but took from the third. God expects us to use what he gives us to benefit his purposes. He rewards those that appreciate and multiply the gifts he gives. He tells us that if we prove to be good caretakers of a little than he will add to our portion. "His lord said unto him, Well done, thou good and faithful servant: thou hast been faithful over a few things, I will make thee ruler over many things: enter thou into the joy of thy lord" (Matt 25:21).

This example gives a look at God's expectation of us. He advocates wise investing in this story. Do not sit on your money. Make it work for you. Be sure the Lord gets his portion. Remember it all belongs to him but he demands tithes and offerings to be given back for his purposes (Mal 3:8).

This analogy stretches beyond our care of the money he provides. It extends to our love and service to others. We are given the fruits of the Spirit (Gal 5:22) and the Lord distributes the gifts of the Spirit according to his will (1 Cor 12). We are not to be complacent with these benefits. Spread them to the rest of the family of God and use them to attract others to him.

Think about what he says in the following verses, "And other fell on good ground, and sprang up, and bare fruit an hundredfold. And when he had said these things, he cried, He that hath ears to hear, let him hear" (Luke 8:8) and in 1 Corinthians 14:12, "Even so ye, forasmuch as ye are zealous of spiritual gifts, seek that ye may excel to the edifying of the church."

Spend time each day remembering what the Lord has done for you through offering free salvation and other things such as breath, food, and water. Show a little appreciation by caring for what he gives. Invest. Grow love, grow peace, grow faith, and grow knowledge.

Week 17

Scripture text—Acts 17:22-23

Then Paul stood in the midst of Mars' hill, and said,
Ye men of Athens, I perceive that in all things ye are too
superstitious. For as I passed by, and beheld your devotions,
I found an altar with this inscription, TO THE UNKNOWN
GOD. Whom therefore ye ignorantly worship, him declare I
unto you.

AT LEAST THE MEN in Athens honored their god with capital letters. This prompted Paul to go on in the following verses to give the truth about the one true God to whom worship must be directed. He created all things. He allows each creature breath, and in him we get our entire substance. He does not *need* anything from us.

He does *want* us to know him and trust him. When I read this section, I thought of the way so many people view God today. They believe in something or someone (they think—not quite sure). I am glad not to live with this vagueness. No wonder people feel a void in their lives. God has given us his Holy Bible for the purpose of knowing him. He also ensures an interest in himself through nature. The things that are seen beckon toward those that are unseen.

No one will have any excuse before him when he asks each for the account of their lives (Rom 1:20).

Anyone that lives in a society knows the difference between an intimate relationship with a loved one and a distant association and/or knowledge of another. To know God exists and to know God are two very different things. Many examples in scripture talk about even devils recognizing Jesus as the holy one but rest assured they are not in his favor.

Claim him for yourself. Read and study scripture, talk to him, rely on him, and learn to trust him. Pay attention to the words of great men of God like David. God called him a *man after his own heart*. That sounds like something to strive for. Read about David in Samuel, Kings, and Chronicles (among other places). He penned many of the Psalms. Start there to learn how the beloved man devoted himself to his master.

Don't just look up and think, *hey up there, anybody home*. Know God and accept his plan of salvation through his son Jesus. Acts 4:12 tells us, "Neither is there salvation in any other: for there is none other name under heaven given among men, whereby we must be saved." It is required to answer his calling, otherwise it will be grim. "And then will I profess unto them, I never knew you: depart from me, ye that work iniquity" (Matt 7:23).

Week 18

Scripture text—Philippians 2:14

Do all things without murmurings and disputings.

THIS IS A TOUGH one. How often do we mumble under our breath when we feel slighted or are not in the mood for the circumstances at hand? Either that or we outwardly (or inwardly) say, but . . . ready to dispute. Sometimes we aren't even reserved about it and lash out in anger.

According to God's Word, these are not correct reactions. Anger in itself is not wrong only how we react to it. "Be ye angry and sin not" (Eph 4:26a). The verse in Philippians is not a passive statement but a command. We must remember that all that faces us has been allowed into our life by God. He gives us the strength to live as servants to him and to others. He will not put us into a situation without also giving us the ability to bear and rise above our immediate/wrongful human nature (1 Cor 10:13).

Pray for faith and wisdom. If prayer is constantly on your tongue it is easier to react according to the Spirit of God. A technique that really works and that he ordains is to live unto him. Acting as a servant and with deference to others is the same as showing deference to him. No one will

Week 18

argue with the wisdom of that. God holds the details of our lives in his hands.

If we are truly being treated poorly, we can trust in him to right the situation. Bring the situation to him in prayer and trust. God is faithful. Consider the following verses. Romans 12:19, "Dearly beloved, avenge not yourselves, but rather give place unto wrath: for it is written, Vengeance is mine; I will repay, saith the Lord," and Deuteronomy 32:35, "To me belongeth vengeance, and recompence; their foot shall slide in due time: for the day of their calamity is at hand, and the things that shall come upon them make haste."

It is difficult to obey God's commands sometimes. Prayer, scripture reading, and practice are the ways to keep spiritual discernment at the forefront throughout your day. Memorize the feature verse.

Here are three others to keep close to your heart and help check your attitude: Colossians 3:23, "And whatsoever ye do, do it heartily, as to the Lord, and not unto men," First Corinthians 10:31, "Whether therefore ye eat, or drink, or whatsoever ye do, do all to the glory of God," and Ephesians 6:7, "With good will doing service, as to the Lord, and not to men."

By keeping the words of God treasured in your heart and available for instant recall, you will more often react in a way that will glorify him, no murmurings or disputings.

Week 19

Scripture text—2 Corinthians 1:21-22

Now he which stablisheth us with you in Christ,
and hath anointed us, is God; Who hath also sealed us,
and given the earnest of the Spirit in our hearts.

MY BIBLE HAS A note next to this verse for the word earnest which says down payment. I had never known that usage before so checked my dictionary. I am ashamed to have lived this long without knowing this meaning of the term. I have always understood earnest to mean to do something with serious purpose.

It also means, a thing intended or regarded as a sign or promise of what is to come—and a reality, first fruits, a part given beforehand as a pledge for the whole as an indication, a token. What a wonderful lesson.

Paul said it beautifully. As Christians, we hold the promise of God's presence with us as the temple of the indwelling Holy Spirit and this is just the beginning of what we can expect as children of the inheritance. We have hope from Isaiah 64:4, "For since the beginning of the world men have not heard, nor perceived by the ear, neither hath the eye seen, O God, beside thee, what he hath prepared for him that waiteth for him" and the reminder in the New Testament in

Week 19

1 Corinthians 2:9, "But as it is written, Eye hath not seen, nor ear heard, neither have entered into the heart of man, the things which God hath prepared for them that love him."

When Christ ascended to Heaven after his resurrection he told the disciples not to fret. He would be back. In the meantime, the Holy Spirit would come as the Comforter to hold us until he returns. John 16:7 says, "Nevertheless I tell you the truth; It is expedient for you that I go away: for if I go not away, the Comforter will not come unto you; but if I depart, I will send him unto you." Hence, the down payment we enjoy until our promise of eternal life with him comes to pass.

The Holy Spirit (also known as the Comforter, the Helper, and the Spirit of Truth) brings many benefits. The fruits of the Spirit can be found in Galatians 5:22. The gifts of the Spirit can be found in 1 Corinthians 12:4–11. These properties are meant for our growth toward the day when we will shrug off our corrupt bodies and mortality (Rom 2:7, 1 Cor 15:53–54). They are also for the edification of one another and as an example to the world.

When our Lord returns we will have been preparing for our incorruptibility/immortality and our union with him through the ministry of conviction and protection of the third person of the Trinity. If we die first, we can be sure our Heaven ready bodies will catch up with us. Consider the scripture, "That there shall be a resurrection of the dead, both of the just and unjust" (Acts 24:15b). We will either get resurrected to life or to damnation (John 5:29).

For those who are redeemed according to belief in Jesus's finished work on the cross, we are established and anointed as saints. Our sins are not counted against us but the penalty paid once and forever by Christ. In the accepting of that fact, we are given our down payment. He is our seal of redemption. Glorify God for his mercy and his Word which he gave us so that we may know these things.

Week 20

Scripture text—Psalms 49:7

None of them can by any means redeem his brother, nor give to God a ransom for him.

God will hold each individual responsible for his/her own choices. Because you have been raised in a Christian family or socialize with Christians does not automatically put you in God's favor. Christianity does not come through osmosis but is a personal condition of the heart. "For the LORD searcheth all hearts, and understandeth all the imaginations of the thoughts: if thou seek him, he will be found of thee; but if thou forsake him, he will cast thee off for ever" (1 Chr 28:9b).

Trying to buy another person's way into Heaven with donations to the church once they are deceased is folly. Their eternal destination is decided (by them) before they pass to the afterlife. "And as it is appointed unto men once to die, but after this the judgment" (Heb 9:27). Read the latter section of Luke chapter 16 for a sharp illustration of this.

Accepting Christ sooner rather than later is a wise choice. A philosopher once reflected that to believe in God is smart because if you believe and he exists than you have done well. If, however, you do not believe and he exists, you have than lost everything and will suffer greatly for it. Why risk it? To turn your back on the gift of eternal life and the benefits of knowing him in this lifetime is self-defeating.

How many years do you have left to live? how many days? minutes? Proverb 27:1 says, "Boast not thyself of to morrow; for thou knowest not what a day may bring forth." The breath you are drawing right now could be your last. Why waste another minute without knowing Jesus Christ. He is not only a nice man that lived long ago but God. "I and my Father are one" (John 10:30).

Reach out to him and accept his gift. Come to him as you are. When God searches the Book of Life, it is your name he will seek. He will not be looking for your family's last name or the name of your church. "And whosoever was not found written in the book of life was cast into the lake of fire" (Rev 20:15).

Humans cannot meet God's holy standard. Through our actions we are all Hell bound. Redemption comes through accepting Jesus's work through the shedding of his blood. He substituted himself to pay our way into Heaven and into a relationship with God.

Don't keep God at a distance. You can know him. It is up to you to decide. No one else can save you by proxy. You will have to face him yourself. "So then every one of us shall give account of himself to God" (Rom 14:12). Jesus is the judge. John 5:22 says, "For the Father judgeth no man, but hath committed all judgment unto the Son."

You do not want him to say "I never knew you: depart from me" (Mathew 7:23b) but rather, "come, ye blessed of my Father, inherit the kingdom" (Matt 25:34b). If you already know Christ, seek to know him better. Pray for others in your life that are wondering but don't feel ready. Be an example to them by loving them. Live love to everyone you come across.

God Likes Ants: Every Week

If you are not a Christian, seek him through scripture and prayer. "All that the Father giveth me shall come to me; and him that cometh to me I will in no wise cast out" (John 6:37). You may not have as much time as you think to decide and why wait for the blessed life that is yours with God by your side.

Week 21

Scripture text—Luke 12:25-26

And which of you with taking thought can add to his stature one cubit? If ye then be not able to do that thing which is least, why take ye thought for the rest?

THIS VERSE IS PERTINENT in today's modern world with so many stressed to the breaking point by worry. This is a sin and a waste of time and energy. Life seems complicated with financial, health, and relationship concerns. It takes practice to settle the natural tendency to wonder what the future holds.

My Father in Heaven knows what I need before I ask him (Matt 6:8). He graciously takes care of even the heathen. "For he maketh his sun to rise on the evil and on the good, and sendeth rain on the just and on the unjust" (Matt 5:45b). I like how he says his sun in that last verse, a reminder that all things are indeed his.

God desires us to rely on him for our needs on a day by day basis. His prayer template in Matthew 6 says to pray each day for our daily bread. Dedicate each day to him and you can be sure that he is faithful to take care of your needs. He knows life can overwhelm us so he instructs us to handle each day separately. Matthew 6:34 says, "Take therefore no thought for the morrow: for the morrow shall take thought for the things of itself. Sufficient unto the day is the evil thereof." He demands faith. "But without faith it is impossible to please him: for he that cometh to God must believe that he is, and that he is a rewarder of them that diligently seek him" (Heb 11:6).

Remember in the desert when God provided the Israelites with manna from Heaven for their food. They were to collect enough to sustain them for one day and no more (except on Sabbath eve when they could collect for two days). If they failed to trust God with fresh provisions for the next day and tried to hoard, he spoiled the extra, making it wormy and inedible to them (Exod 16:20).

God expects us to trust him. He repeats over and again in his Word that we must live by faith. What is faith? His own definition is in Hebrews 11:1, "Now faith is the substance of things hoped for, the evidence of things not seen." Faith can be hard but it can be practiced and nurtured. The more you put your life in God's hands, the more you will learn that he is faithful and worthy of trust. A life rich in prayer and fasting will increase faith (Matt 17:20–21). Let the Creator handle the details of your days and go forth with peace in your heart.

Week 22

Scripture text—Revelation 2:17

He that hath an ear, let him hear what the Spirit saith unto the churches; To him that overcometh will I give to eat of the hidden manna, and will give him a white stone, and in the stone a new name written, which no man knoweth saving he that receiveth it.

Parents spend so much time deciding and even argue over what to name their new bundle of joy as the birth date approaches. As a child I did not like my name and had a list of potential changes lined up. I grew to love the name but now I am excited to get my white stone. I will learn my real name. Real because it comes from God and will last throughout eternity, aren't you curious?

God knew everything about us before we were born (Jer 1:5) and he had our spirit ready to join our physical bodies. Just like long after we die he will resurrect our bodies in a condition fit for Heaven. He knows our name. What a bond we will share with our Savior.

Manna is the bread of Heaven. The Israelites called it manna because they did not know what else to call it. They described it as "like coriander seed, white and tasted like wafers made with honey" (Exod 16:15, 31). Those of us that belong to him will eat of hidden manna. I bet he adds chocolate to this manna. There is so much to look forward to as God welcomes us to partake of his mysteries.

The verse mentions the message is for those who have ears to hear. John 8:47 says, "He that is of God heareth God's words: ye therefore hear them not, because ye are not of God." Not everyone can grasp the words of God because they are not his. The misnomer that everyone is God's child is a dangerous teaching. John 8:44 grimly says, "Ye are of your father the devil, and the lusts of your father ye will do. He was a murderer from the beginning, and abode not in the truth, because there is no truth in him. When he speaketh a lie, he speaketh of his own: for he is a liar, and the father of it." God knows his own children: we can hear, we can see, and we will overcome. "My sheep hear my voice, and I know them, and they follow me" (John 10:27).

Get excited about eternity. If you hear his voice, go to him. Like Jacob that God renamed Israel, Simon who God renamed Peter, and Saul who God renamed Paul, your new name will be presented to you by Jesus on your very own white stone. It will be very bright up there with the shining glory of God, all those white robes, and white stones. "This then is the message which we have heard of him, and declare unto you, that God is light, and in him is no darkness at all" (1 John 1:5).

Week 23

Scripture text—Proverbs 3:5-6

Trust in the LORD with all thine heart; and lean not unto thine own understanding. In all thy ways acknowledge him, and he shall direct thy paths.

If we seek to lean on something we search for rest or support. The scope of the human experience is too small to adequately meet these needs. Other people are just as flawed as we are so while they can temporarily offer a leaning post, they will eventually get weak and fall too. We look to our past and the circumstances around us to provide our understanding. We read many books and have discussions with smart people trying to boost our understanding. Important as these measures are, they cannot come near the vastness of God's resources.

We learn from King Solomon in Proverbs 4:7 that, "Wisdom is the principle thing; therefore get wisdom: and with all thy getting get understanding." You may be thinking I would love to go to the store and pick up a case of wisdom and understanding. That is a parody of thinking we can provide our own. Just pay the money. Instead remember that, "A man can receive nothing, except it be given him from heaven" (John 3:27b).

God Likes Ants: Every Week

First Kings 4:29 tells us that God gave Solomon wisdom and understanding. James, Jesus's brother said, "If any of you lack wisdom, let him ask of God, that giveth to all men liberally, and upbraideth not; and it shall be given him" (Jas 1:5).

Prayer is the answer. Develop an intimate relationship with the Creator and sustainer of all things. In him is where rest and support are found. Like all principles of Christianity, learning to acknowledge God through prayer takes faith, trust, and practice. The more examples you learn of his faithfulness, the less you will worry about your path. Acknowledge him in your finances by tithing. Thank him throughout each day for all of your basic provisions plus all the bonus gifts he throws in. Tell family, friends, and co-workers about Jesus and live to honor him. He promises that if we do so that he will direct our paths. I like the idea of God as my personal director. No longer do I have to wonder what the correct course is. If I do my part, he will do his. Hebrews 10:23b says, "For he is faithful that promised." You can't go wrong if you make it your goal to "Pray without ceasing" (1 Thess 5:17). Pull up a seat in the throne room and make yourself comfortable. Better yet, get on your knees.

Week 24

Scripture text—Proverbs 14:12

There is a way which seemeth right unto a man,
but the end thereof are the ways of death.

The trouble with many people today is they believe if they just do their best in life that God could not ask for more. The truth is that God is just and his standard is high, perfection. The Bible teaches that all have come short of the glory of God (Rom 3:23); all have sinned and all are worthy of death.

We were created as a species to live in perfect communion with God but through Adam's sin all became guilty. Such the same as all that accept Christ can regain life eternal. Romans 5:12 says, "Wherefore, as by one man sin entered into the world, and death by sin; and so death passed upon all men [women too], for that all have sinned." Through his mercy he sent his son, Jesus, to provide a substitute for our place in death. Isaiah 53 is an amazing prophecy of Christ written 700 years before his time spent on earth. I urge everyone to read the whole chapter. Verses 5–6 serve as a snapshot of his mission, "But he was wounded for our transgressions, he was bruised for our iniquities: the chastisement of our peace was upon him; and with his stripes we are healed. All we like sheep have gone astray; we have turned everyone to his own way; and the LORD hath laid on him the iniquity of us all."

People must understand that we are born with the sinful nature. So if it seems natural it could be the opposite of what God wants. It is vital to be born again, born of the Spirit (read John 3). The third person of the Holy Trinity indwells the believer and brings a new way of looking at all things. The natural tendency is not to be trusted much of the time. Trust God. You will read in 1 Corinthians 2:14, "But the natural man receiveth not the things of the Spirit of God: for they are foolishness unto him: neither can he know them, because they are spiritually discerned."

The way to gain eternal life in Heaven (all have eternal life—but where is it spent?) is to believe in Jesus's finished work on the cross. God loves when people do good things, but sin always happens with all the doing. John tells the truth in his Gospel message, "Then said they unto him, what shall we do, that we might work the works of God? Jesus answered and said unto them, This is the work of God, that ye believe on him whom he hath sent" (John 6:28–29). All of the things we do to try to get ourselves into God's good graces except trust Jesus are folly. He wants us to do good things but as a byproduct of our salvation. As Paul taught the Ephesians, so we should remember, "For by grace are ye saved through faith; and that not of yourselves: it is the gift of God: Not of works, lest any man should boast" (Eph 2:8–9).

Trust Jesus and afterwards use good works as praise, worship, and thanksgiving for the gifts he so freely gives. Remember the natural man/woman is not in God's favor. Learn God's personality through studying scripture and constantly communicating with him. God does not change. While we are not subject to the laws in the Old Testament, it is a place to learn what he likes and what displeases him. Don't lose sight of Jesus by becoming too legalistic but strive to know God as well as possible. Much he reserves as a mystery for us to learn in our afterlife.

A verse that comforts, extols, and instructs is Isaiah 55:8. It says, "For my thoughts are not your thoughts, neither are your ways my ways, saith the LORD." This helps us to give all things up to him. He is above all and his ways lead to life. Christians mature through commitment to Jesus and over time develop the very mind of Christ (1 Cor 2:16). This should be your goal. Over time it will get easier to please God and know his ways. You need him to avoid the ways to death.

Week 25

Scripture text—Romans 1:19-20

Because that which may be known of God is manifest in them; for God hath shewed it unto them. For the invisible things of him from the creation of the world are clearly seen, being understood by the things that are made, even his eternal power and Godhead; so that they are without excuse.

GOD PROGRAMS THE KNOWLEDGE of his existence into each creature. To manifest something is to make it clear to the understanding, to show plainly, or to prove. Our bodies are a part of the energy cycle which is essentially dirt rearranged but our spirits come from God (Eccl 12:7). He planned each of our unique personalities and like a computer that comes with hardware already installed, God has hard wired us to seek after him.

In Psalms 19:1-3, David tells it beautifully, "The heavens declare the glory of God; and the firmament sheweth his handywork. Day unto day uttereth speech, and night unto night sheweth knowledge. There is no speech nor language, where their voice is not heard."

Except when the Lord stopped the sun and the moon for a day for Joshua's plea, the cycle of day and night continues as ordained by God (Josh 10:12-14). All people have experience with astronomy as with the natural sciences of geology, chemistry, biology, and hydrology simply through the miracle of being alive. Forgive me if I have left off your favorite branch of study.

Science is fascinating. It is foolish to believe that God and science are at odds. God is the ultimate scientist. When people study science they are studying God. Too bad many fail to give him the credit for all of it. It is a matter of worshiping the creation instead of the Creator.

Romans 1:25 reminds us that God knew people would reject him in favor of the works of his Word. It says, "Who changed the truth of God into a lie, and worshipped and served the creature [creation] more than the Creator, who is blessed forever. Amen." Have you considered the word universe? Breaking it down it tells much: uni=One, verse=expression. God said it and it was so.

The things of God are clearly seen and understood by that which is made. Look no further than the trees and flowers in your yard, the ants at your picnic, the rocks on the ground, the rivers, the stars, and your own body's functioning to see God's eternal power. Unfortunately most people through pride and idolatry become indifferent or hostile to the evident truth in God's revelation.

It is through this hardness of heart that God withdraws from some people. Ephesians 4:17–18 tells it like this, "This I say therefore, and testify in the Lord, that ye henceforth walk not as other Gentiles walk, in the vanity of their mind, having the understanding darkened, being alienated from the life of God through the ignorance that is in them, because of the blindness of their heart." Conversely, the good news is that if you "Draw nigh to God, he will draw nigh to you" (Jas 4:8a).

No one will be justified by answering God with *I never even heard of you*. When questioned have the correct answer. Jesus paid it all. To him goes the credit. Study scripture and nature to know God. His imagination knows no bounds, enjoy.

Week 26

Scripture text—Mark 7:6b-7

This people honoureth me with their lips, but their heart is far from me. Howbeit in vain do they worship me, teaching for doctrines the commandments of men.

ARE YOU GUILTY OF vain repetitions? Matthew said in his Gospel that going through the familiar motions of prayer will not necessarily promote your voice to God. Prayer, worshipful singing, and even broadcasting the Gospel are pointless unless you love the Lord. When spending time with him give him your full attention. He does not want the back seat of our affections.

He wants our devotion: heart, soul, mind, and strength (Mark 12:30). In Luke 10:27, in the almost identical command, we get the added message to love our neighbor as ourselves. That is harder than loving God. It is a command, though, and we have to take our best shot.

Like many people, I recite the Lord's Prayer daily. It is hanging on my wall just like it was when I was a child. My dad taught me many good habits. Jesus gave us the template (Matt 6:9-13) and said, "After this manner therefore pray" (9a). In some church services, oral exchanges are used as a routine. These are vain babblings when the droning speakers are thinking of the stack of laundry at home, the afternoon football game, the fight with their son, and all else except the God they are pretending to worship. God tries the heart (1 Thess 2:4). Do not approach him without proper reverence and relationship. It is a waste of energy. An example of those that act complacently is found in Matthew 7:21–23:

> Not everyone that saith unto me, Lord, Lord, shall enter into the kingdom of heaven; but he that doeth the will of my Father which is in heaven. Many will say to me in that day, Lord, Lord, have we not prophesied in thy name? and in thy name have cast out devils? and in thy name done many wonderful works? And then will I profess unto them, I never knew you: depart from me, ye that work iniquity.

That takes us to the next point in the featured verse. Often, and more frequently as the end gets nearer, false doctrines are making their way into mainstream Christianity. Never mind the apostasy found in whole sects of Christians, the once reliable churches are teaching doctrines to please people and not the truth of God.

The coexist movement are joined by end times date guessing (Matt 24:36) and all manner of spiritualism. Accepting people and loving them are a command from God, but static sinful behaviors must not be condoned (Rom 1:25–32).

Know the scriptures. Study them like your life depends on it because it does. If you know what God's word says you will know when you hear a false teaching. Paul repeats himself directly in Galatians 1:8–9, "But though we, or an angel from heaven, preach any other gospel unto you than that which we have preached unto you, let him be accursed. As we said before, so say I now again, if any man preach any other gospel unto you than that ye have received, let him be accursed." First John 4:1b tells us to "try the spirits whether they are of God: because many false prophets are gone out into the world."

False teachings can result from liberal translations. Many Bibles that claim to be the truth have changed vital language in the text to be more pleasing to modern readers. This is about man/woman wanting to be his/her own god, beware. Compare any version to King James or an older version if you can find one. It is an interesting study for comparison. People have become linguistically lazy. King James is easy to grasp with a pinpoint of dedication. I offer kudos to those who study the original languages.

God will have the final word as the following verses from the last verses of the canon show. Revelation 22:18–19 settles it:

> For I testify unto every man that heareth the words of the prophecy of this book, If any man shall add unto these things, God shall add unto him the plagues that are written in this book: And if any man shall take away from the words of the book of this prophecy, God shall take away his part out of the book of life, and out of the holy city, and from the things which are written in this book.

So put your heart in the right place when praying to the Creator. Let your words be heard. Know his truth so you can sort out the weeds that pass for Bible teachings. You must have a standard, make it the Lord's own inspired words (2 Tim 3:16).

Week 27

Scripture text—Ecclesiastes 9:10a

Whatsoever thy hand findeth to do, do it with thy might.

It was my earthy father that first taught me to do things right the first time and I wouldn't have to do them twice. I remember him sending my sister and I to polish the dressers again if his inspection found our efforts lacking. He checked behind our ears and in the bend of our arms for dirt after the bath. We soaked again and used soap the second time. I am not sure how long it took me to get the message.

The phrase *do it right or don't do it at all* seemed like a great way to get out of chores. In fact, the trick did relieve me of dish duty at holiday meals. I still hate doing dishes having resorted to paying the teenager upstairs to wash my sink full.

My dad knew the scriptures before I did. He taught me principles that I have grown to cherish. His example rubbed off on me as I often remember his motto, keep the faith.

A long time removed from the daily lessons from dad, they help me to remember that it is my Father in Heaven who I must please. Colossians 3:23 says, "And whatsoever ye do, do it heartily, as to the Lord, and not unto men." Ants are a good example of diligence. Consider my title verse. Consider the way ants work together and give full effort to meeting goals. The little critters not only enlist their [hands] with all their might but their mouths and bodies too.

"The hand of the diligent shall bear rule: but the slothful shall be under tribute" (Prov 12:24). Noah of Genesis used diligence and mighty faith when he constructed the ark. He and his family alone survived the flood and everyone else paid for their actions with death. "All in whose nostrils was the breath of life, of all that was in dry land, died" (Gen 7:22).

Imagine the faith Noah had. All the people watching him prepare the ark and the animals ridiculed him yet he believed God. In so doing, his faith saved him. There was much work involved in building the ark, gathering the animals . . . imagine the logistics.

Each of us will probably never have to undertake such a vast project. Scripture tells us that we are to do our best in whatever we do. Honor God in all things and remember to thank him for the means to do that.

Week 28

Scripture text—Philippians 1:6

Being confident of this very thing, that he which hath begun a good work in you will perform it until the day of Jesus Christ.

CONFIDENCE CAN BE ILLUSIVE in the modern age. Changes disrupt our families, our jobs, and our health. Praise to God that he is above our circumstances. Christians are promised that when he takes us on as a project that he does not abandon it. We are being groomed by our Father for eternity in Heaven. We are to obey God through practicing the guidance in his Word, acting according to the conviction of the Holy Spirit, and keeping him in the fore of our thoughts as he teaches us how to be like Christ. Eternal life starts here and now.

God does not call us to a terrible life. It is his plan to lead us through green meadows and beside still waters (Ps 23:2). If we decide to ignore him and play with the world, he will teach us valuable lessons. It is to our benefit and through it all, he is with us. Embrace him.

Life can be lived confidently and victoriously. Help yourself by wearing the full armour of God. Our own flesh vexes us with its sinful nature but Satan does much to turn us from the correct way. Ephesians 6:11–17 tells us how to fight:

God Likes Ants: Every Week

> Put on the whole armour of God, that ye may be able to stand against the wiles of the devil. For we wrestle not against flesh and blood, but against principalities, against powers, against the rulers of the darkness of this world, against spiritual wickedness in high places. Wherefore take unto you the whole armour of God, that ye may be able to withstand in the evil day, and having done all, to stand. Stand therefore, having your loins girt about with truth, and having on the breastplate of righteousness; And your feet shod with the preparation of the gospel of peace; Above all, taking the shield of faith, wherewith ye shall be able to quench all the fiery darts of the wicked. And take the helmet of salvation, and the sword of the Spirit, which is the word of God.

He offers us a lot of protection, why not use it. Things will happen that seem like setbacks to our growth but faith insists that we believe God. Hebrews 11:6a says, "But without faith it is impossible to please him."

Own peace: "And we know that all things work together for good to them that love God, to them who are the called according to his purpose" (Rom 8:28).

Week 29

Scripture text—Luke 24:39

Behold my hands and my feet, that it is I myself:
handle me, and see; for a spirit hath not flesh and bones,
as ye see me have.

THE FIRST STORY I remember about what would happen to me once I made it to Heaven would be that I would get wings and become an angel. I believed for a long time that once my body was in the grave, that was the end of it, and I would be floating through eternity as a spirit/angel. It is understandable that adults give children simple answers, as long as the child is directed to the Bible for full disclosure. Interest is piqued and the truth is known through studying God's own guide to us.

I now know that we are entirely different creations with different roles and niches in God's sovereign plan. We will judge the angels and thank God that human beings have the option to be redeemed, a gift unavailable to the angels.

While I am anxious to cast off this wretched human flesh which I often feel powerless to control, God will resurrect this pity into a fit for Heaven immortal incapable of sin. Jesus was the first of the resurrected (of course he and the faithful did raise people from the dead, but those died again to await the resurrection of the dead which is before the great judgment). John 5:28–29 says, "Marvel not at this: for the hour is coming, in the which all that are in the graves shall hear his voice, And shall come forth; they that have done good, unto the resurrection of life; and they that have done evil, unto the resurrection of damnation." When Jesus's disciples doubted his reality after that first Easter, he evidenced himself as flesh and bone. They laid hands on him and ate with him. By believing the Gospel of Christ we will gain perfect bodies to live in a perfect state with no sin and no want.

All saints that have gone before are in spirit waiting for their bodies to be made perfect when they will reunite with them. A few thousand years is not long to wait when compared to eternity. Enoch and Elijah have never seen physical death as their special ordaining from God. The same is true for the Christians alive when God proclaims the harvest of the saints at the rapture.

The righteous will live through eternity as real people. "So when this corruptible shall have put on incorruption, and this mortal shall have put on immortality, then shall be brought to pass the saying that is written, Death is swallowed up in victory" (1 Cor 15:54). Watch.

Week 30

Scripture text—Zechariah 12:9

And it shall come to pass in that day, that I will seek to destroy all the nations that come against Jerusalem.

"The LORD of hosts shall defend them" (Zech 9:15a). It gets wearisome listening to people discuss the animosity in the Middle East between Israel and almost all other nations in that region. The clash goes all the way back to Genesis. The children of Abraham claim rights to all that land; however, the promise continued through Isaac and Jacob (renamed Israel by God). The land belongs to Israel.

The story of Sarah (mother of Isaac) and Hagar (mother of Ishmael) can be read in Genesis chapter 16. References abound throughout scripture with the assurance that the true God is the God of Abraham, Isaac, and Israel. The fight between these relatives will not cease through any attempt made by us humans.

Galatians says in 4:22–23, "For it is written, that Abraham had two sons, the one by a bondmaid [Hagar], the other by a freewoman [Sarah]. But he who was of the bondwoman was born after the flesh; but he of the freewoman was by promise." And further in 4:29, "But as then he that was born after the flesh persecuted him that was born after the Spirit, even so it is now."

God Likes Ants: Every Week

We know from Bible study that the flesh must be redeemed by the Spirit in order to live. "Verily, verily, I say unto thee, Except a man be born of water and of the Spirit, he cannot enter into the kingdom of heaven. That which is born of the flesh is flesh; and that which is born of the Spirit is spirit" (John 3:5–6).

Jerusalem is God's chosen city as Israel is his chosen people. "And unto his son will I give one tribe, that David my servant may have a light alway before me in Jerusalem, the city which I have chosen me to put my name there" (1 Kgs 11:36). Jesus came from the line of David (Judah). To study Jesus's lineage see Luke chapter 3 and Matthew chapter 1.

Nations that seek to destroy Israel with be destroyed by God. The United States cannot abandon Israel because to do so is to abandon God. The predicament is above human economics, sociology, and politics. It is God's politics. The script is written. God and his people win.

When Jesus Christ comes again to rescue Israel from her enemies, the Jews will recognize him as the one rejected as the Messiah by Israel when he was crucified. Thank God that he was though, so we can live through a relationship with him. "Salvation is of the Jews," says John 4:22b. Through God's mercy he made a plan to include the rest of us through adoption into the family. This adoption comes from accepting Christ's gift. The gift is eternal life through belief.

Israel will recognize Jesus upon his arrival and the Bible says that when they see that it is Jesus they will mourn for him and for the knowledge of what his presence on earth meant. Consider the three verses below:

> Zechariah 12:10—And I will pour upon the house of David, and upon the inhabitants of Jerusalem, the spirit of grace and of supplications: and they shall look upon me whom they have pierced, and they shall mourn for him, as

Week 30

one mourneth for his only son, and shall be in bitterness for him, as one that is in bitterness for his firstborn. John 19:37—And again another scripture saith, They shall look on him whom they pierced. Revelation 1:7—Behold he cometh with clouds; and every eye shall see him, and they also which pierced him: and all kindreds of the earth shall wail because of him. Even so, Amen.

Study scripture. God has given us his Word so we may know what is to come. As an individual, seek to know Christ. Pray for Israel and that the government of the United States will never waiver in supporting God's people.

Week 31

Scripture text—Proverbs 27:1

Boast not thyself of to morrow; for thou knoweth not what a day may bring forth.

MEMORIZING THIS VERSE HAS helped me to remember the importance of living by faith. It is hard to not project forward to what will happen next year, next month, or tomorrow. In truth we know nothing of what will be. I am guilty of saying, *in a month, I will do this or that*. What a presumptuous attitude. Then I look the fool when my plans fail. Best to give way to Gods plans, they are foolproof.

The future lies in the will of God. He must spend much time giggling (or crying) at our plans. He knows we are perhaps way off and sad because we don't trust him to take care of it for us. If we follow him we can rest assured whatever tomorrow holds will benefit us. Paul says in Romans, "And we know that all things work together for good to them that love God, to them who are the called according to his purpose" (8:28).

A day is the measure of time to be concerned with. The Lord's Prayer reminds us to ask God to provide us with daily bread. Are your needs met for the day you are living in? Do not fear where your provisions will come from

Week 31

henceforth. If you love God, he will be sure you are cared for, and abundantly. We lose sight of appreciating the gifts of the day if our attention is focused elsewhere. I think of this concept often when watching people in the modern age constantly with their attention on electronic devices while beauty and life happen before their eyes if only they would look up and maybe even listen.

Treat every day like the gift that it is. It could be like the story of the man who wanted to build bigger barns for his gains, "But God said unto him, Thou fool, this night thy soul shall be required of thee: then whose shall those things be, which thou hast provided?" (Luke 12:20). Not only is God saying that to build up material goods is folly because earthly death can arrive at any time but also that it is folly for another reason. Who knows what will happen to your goods when you die? Who knows if your children will care for them or lose them foolishly? This is a topic spoken of much by Solomon in Ecclesiastes.

The best advice for living on earth is to know Christ and pray constantly for guidance. "Trust in the LORD with all thine heart; and lean not unto thine own understanding. In all thy ways acknowledge him, and he shall direct thy paths" (Prov 3:5–6).

Don't miss out on the joys of each day. Live slower. If you are looking forward it should be to eternity. You have to spend it somewhere. Up or down? Be ready.

Week 32

Scripture text—Hebrews 13:16

But to do good and to communicate forget not:
for with such sacrifices God is well pleased.

What do you consider a sacrifice in your life? canceling the cable to save money in today's economy? ordering a plain tea at the coffee shop instead of a latte? using public transportation instead of a personal car to cut back?

Let's remember that in our experience these seem like actions that take commitment and resolve but to most people globally the result of our sacrifices are still a luxury. Not much of a sacrifice at all if we get our perspective straight.

The above are good ideas for living simpler which God likes but he knows that small acts of kindness take effort for us. "There is none that doeth good, no, not one" (Pss 14:3b, 53:3b, Rom 3:12b). He brings this message home by repeating it three times throughout the Bible. Also Psalms 103:14 says, "For he knoweth our frame; he remembereth that we are dust."

God's big thing is to love your neighbor as yourself. "For all the law is fulfilled in one word, even in this; Thou shall love thy neighbor as thyself" (Gal 5:14). To love one's neighbor is difficult especially in light of the truth Jeremiah

Week 32

reflects in 17:9. "The heart is deceitful above all things, and desperately wicked: who can know it?"

Why not give a nod of understanding to the rushed mother at the grocery that cuts in line instead of a scowl and scathing remarks under your breath? Hand a bill to a street person. It is easy to judge them but God will take our charity and carry it forward. He will reward you openly for good acts you perform in secret (Matt 6:4).

Guard your thoughts and actions. Take the right course according to Jesus's example in the Gospels. God realizes that we are not disposed to kindness, sharing, and compromise. To him, what we dismiss as trivial daily interactions, he sees as an opportunity to sacrifice our human nature to please him.

We are brought to life through the greatest sacrifice, Jesus's death at Calvary. Make your own sacrifices to show appreciation for that gift and fulfill his desire for us. The sacrifice it takes to deny our selfishness and love others.

Week 33

Scripture text—Isaiah 65:24

And it shall come to pass, that before they call, I will answer; and while they are yet speaking, I will hear.

Prayer is important for communion with God. It is as simple as talking to the person next to you, after all he is there. It comes in many forms but does not have to be structured. Like any conversation with a friend, say whatever is on your mind. He knows what you are thinking anyway. He delights to be included in our daily lives. Not just for petitions and praises but what we are thinking about and doing on any given day.

First Thessalonians 5:17 says, "Pray without ceasing." I find this difficult when I am engaged in a project or out enjoying time with friends. I realize after a few hours that I miss the Lord. He is forever present with me but I often have to make a conscious effort to keep him *in the loop* of my life. That is the way to ensure that all will go well with me. "In all thy ways acknowledge him, and he shall direct thy paths" (Proverb 3:6).

Like any relationship, the more communication shared between parties the better. Jesus gave the example we call the Lord's Prayer in Matthew 6:9–13. Prayer is a way

Week 33

to show your trust in God. Let him know that you want and need his involvement in everything. It is true we can do nothing without him, so remember to thank him.

A favorite example relating to the week's feature is found in Daniel 10:12-13, "Then said he unto me, fear not Daniel: for from the first day that thou didst set thine heart to understand, and to chasten thyself before thy God, thy words were heard, and I am come for thy words. But the prince of the kingdom of Persia withstood me one and twenty days: but, lo, Michael, one of the chief princes, came to help me; and I remained there with the kings of Persia."

Daniel's prayers were heard and responded to as soon as he set his petition in his heart. An important part of the above piece of Daniel is that it reminds us how the prince of the air (Satan) works to hinder God's work. After God sent an angel to visit Daniel with his answer to prayer, the angel was delayed because of a fight with the dark side en route for three weeks. The struggle required Michael himself to come to the aid of the lesser angel, the message carrier.

Don't give God the silent treatment. Seek him for everything. Wait patiently for his answers; it could be that his messengers are fighting to get to your ear. Remember too that the answer God sends may not be what you had in mind. Trust him.

Week 34

Scripture text—Psalms 118:18

The LORD hath chastened me sore:
but he hath not given me over unto death.

THIS VERSE FORCES US to bring our circumstances into perspective. The Lord does things in our lives and we are sure he has abandoned us. He never does. Consider the book of Job. It helps when I want to complain about a lesson the Lord is teaching me or to just accept his sovereignty.

When we are walking a path that we know we should not then we can expect some correction from our Lord. "As many as I love, I rebuke and chasten: be zealous therefore, and repent" (Rev 3:19). The best answer to reduce unfavorable consequences is to remain in a state of grace with God.

Do this through asking him for guidance in all things. Nothing is too small to take to him. He cares and wants to know that we lean on him, as a child. Luke 18:17 tells us how serious he is about putting complete trust in him, "Verily I say unto you, Whosoever shall not receive the kingdom of God as a little child shall in no wise enter therein."

When you sin ask him to pardon you. If you are already a Christian, than your salvation is secure but unconfessed sin will certainly lead him to action. Don't let it build up, talk to him always. "If we confess our sins, he is faithful and just to forgive us our sins, and to cleanse us from all unrighteousness" (1 John 1:9).

From experience I can say that when I start to sin, I often forget the Lord and one sin leads to another. At that point I feel awkward approaching him. Don't let it reach that point. He loves us and wants the best for us. Just at this point when your bad behaviors are piling up and you turn from the Lord due to shame or pride, he will chastise you. Leviticus 26:27-28 is clear, "And if ye will not for all this hearken unto me, but walk contrary unto me; Then I will walk contrary unto you also in fury; and I, even I, will chastise you seven times for your sins."

Don't worry. We may be sore when he is through with us, but remember those redeemed in Christ's blood will never die. I call Job to mind again. After he lost all, his wife advised him to curse God and die. Job wisely answered that he would receive good and evil at the hand of God. (Job 2:9-10). He understood God's sovereignty.

It is not hard to know what he wants from us. It is written in his Holy Word. It is not hard to know when we as individuals are displeasing him. The Spirit within us lets us know. We can't escape it, our actions have consequences. "For whom the Lord loveth he chasteneth, and scourgeth every son whom he receiveth" (Heb 12:6).

If you are in the midst of a challenge where God is chastising you for something, learn from the experience and look forward to the peace that will come afterward. "Now no chastening for the present seemeth to be joyous, but grievous: nevertheless afterward it yielded the peaceable fruit of righteousness unto them which are exercised thereby" (Heb 12:11).

He will take you to the edge of the cliff but will not let you fall off. He is working to make us perfect and Heaven ready one day at a time.

Week 35

Scripture text—2 Corinthians 11:3

But I fear, lest by any means, as the serpent beguiled Eve through his subtilty, so your minds should be corrupted from the simplicity that is in Christ.

THE SERPENT'S BEGUILING OF Eve is recorded in Genesis chapter 3. Satan wanted to destroy God's new creation, human beings, from obeying and having sweet communion with their Lord. He had rebelled, been thrown from glory, and now wanted to mess everything up. His reason was pride. Isaiah records in 14:12–14 "How art thou fallen from heaven, O Lucifer, son of the morning . . . For thou hast said in thine heart, I will ascend into heaven, I will exalt my throne above the stars of God . . . I will be like the most High."

He has been a stunning success in messing things up, leading millions to follow him into damnation. He will never be like God, what a fantasy. Satan is the father of lies (John: 8:44) and God cannot lie (Heb 6:18). God has prepared Hell for the devil and his angels, but unsaved people will join them there right after the final judgment. Read the story in Revelation 20:10–15. It begins, "And the devil that deceived them . . ."

Week 35

Satan and his buddies try to cozy up to us in a pretty package and with seemingly innocent suggestions. They can be what we might call big (my spouse will never know about this, anyway—what she/he doesn't know won't hurt) or small (it's just a few packages of paper, the company owes me anyway). In all events, any actions we take will be brought under God's scrutiny. Solomon writes in Ecclesiastes 12:14, "For God shall bring every work into judgment, with every secret thing, whether it be good, or whether it be evil."

Remember that God created Satan to be very beautiful. It is simple for him to make his lies appear beautiful too. "And no marvel; for Satan himself is transformed into an angel of light. Therefore it is no great thing if his ministers also be transformed as the ministers of righteousness; whose end shall be according to their works" (2 Cor 11:14–15). A clear example of this is when Jesus became angry in the temple and lectured the scribes and Pharisees. Even the trusted religious leaders had it wrong. The scourging is too long to reproduce here but please enjoy it in Matthew chapter 23. He was warning them of the consequences of leading others into damnation.

What's a person to do to discern the good from the bad? It is often difficult. Satan gets into our minds and we have to cast him away. Even Peter was unaware when Satan tried to use him to prevent Christ from going to the cross. Matthew 16:23 records, "But he turned, and said unto Peter, Get thee behind me, Satan: thou art an offense unto me: for thou savourest not the things that be of God, but those that be of men." Satan knew that Jesus planned on providing a plan of redemption and he was against it. He wants everyone to suffer his fate.

We must wear the whole armour of God: truth, righteousness, the Gospel, faith, salvation, the Spirit, and the

Word of God (Eph 6:11–17). Accept that you need Jesus to save you and then stick close to him. The people of the world are controlled by Satan and he loves to use Christians to grieve his enemy, Jesus Christ. Get on the winning side because if you follow Satan you are following a liar. Here Paul clearly talks about how we are to be different from the world, "Wherein in time past, ye walked according to the course of this world, according to the prince of the power of the air, the spirit that now worketh in the children of disobedience" (Eph 2:2).

James 4:7 is good advice, "Submit yourselves therefore to God. Resist the devil, and he will flee from you." Resist is an active verb.

Week 36

Scripture text—Job 19:25-26

For I know that my redeemer liveth, and that he shall stand at the latter day upon the earth: and though after my skin worms destroy this body, yet in my flesh shall I see God.

MANY BIBLE SCHOLARS BELIEVE that the book of Job is the oldest book in the Bible. It is among the first no doubt. How exciting to hear Job refer to the latter days. Scripture is inspired by God and the Bible is his textbook to us. While the words are on the page, they are meant to speak. God has always spoken to men's hearts. He also at times whispers in their ears (1 Sam 9:15).

The message of the Resurrection is loud and clear here in Job's words. He had the same hope which keeps Christians of today looking skyward. Jesus is the king and he will rule his kingdom on this earth after he halts the nonsensical mess that Satan has made of things. "Behold, he cometh with clouds; and every eye shall see him, and they also which pierced him: and all kindreds of the earth shall wail because of him. Even so, Amen," said John the blessed in Revelation 1:7.

Keep in mind that Jesus is the second person of the eternal Godhead and that he lived in Heaven throughout eternity past before his appearance in a manger in Bethlehem 2000 odd years ago. He ascended to Heaven after his resurrection that first Easter season and will pop back in on us again when the ordained time arrives.

This refers of course to the second coming of our Savior to earth. At that time those of us who are believers prior to this will come with him having been removed from the wrath of God before the seven years of the tribulation. This removal most people call the rapture. Latter day prophecy is exciting and deserves to be studied at length. We can know. He told us what to expect. Seek and you shall find the answers in scripture.

The people of the earth will mourn at his coming because the day of reckoning will be at hand before Jesus takes his rightful place as king of this planet. It is after his earthly kingdom that all people will be resurrected and face the Creator in their fleshly bodies. Individuals will either be welcomed into Heaven or exiled to Hell forever.

Will you be glad to see him? or worried? "It is a fearful thing to fall into the hands of the living God" (Heb 10:31).

Week 37

Scripture text—Ephesians 5:20

Giving thanks always for all things into God and the Father in the name of our Lord Jesus Christ.

It is the time of the year set aside as Thanksgiving. The scripture above reminds us that every day should be the day to thank God for his provision. People tend to forget and take for granted things in life that are indeed given us through his grace and mercy. Things like breath, food, and shelter come to mind but let us not forget the rest.

The American holiday of Thanksgiving should absolutely bring thanks to God that we are in America where food is plenty. Remember those around the world (and at home too) in prayer this season because most will not have turkey, potatoes, and pie. Most will be grateful if they have bread and some will struggle to have enough water to drink. I can think of a lot of reasons to thank God that I was born in America. Remember to pray for our blessed country. With the climate of the world stage, she needs God's touch more than ever. Don't forget to pray for Israel too.

Most of us can say that we awoke in a comfortable bed today, than set to starting our days with plumbing that works, and any number of luxuries. All things come to us from above. "Every good gift and every perfect gift is from above, and cometh down from above from the Father of lights" (Jas 1:17a). Even things that we can't immediately see as good should be appreciated as his method of leading us toward himself. "And we know that all things work together for good to them that love God, to them who are the called according to his purpose" (Rom 8:28).

Remember Job who chastened his wife that God provided the good and the bad and who are we to complain about it. After he lost all earthly things he said, "Blessed be the name of the LORD" (Job 1:21b). I invite you to look around your room right now and identify what you have to be thankful to God for in just this minute alone. I list my computer, my warm sweater, cup of warm tea, calculator, pictures of family and friends, those very people in my life, electricity, eyes that can see, curtains, literacy, my house plants, and the list goes on.

I got it all from God. He simply wants to be acknowledged and invited into our daily lives. Psalms 95:2 says, "Let us come before his presence with thanksgiving, and make a joyful noise unto him with psalms." You can speak your thanks in prayer silently or as the Psalmist recommends . . . sing—sing—sing. You don't have to sound like a song bird for God to hear you and count it as worship.

Even Jesus thanked his Father. Jesus's words in John 11: 41b are, "Father, I thank thee that thou hast heard me." Keep God always in the forefront of your mind. Keep praise and a thank you on your lips. Happy Thanksgiving to all.

Week 38

Scripture text—2 Thessalonians 3:6

Now we command you, brethren, in the name of our Lord Jesus Christ, that ye withdraw yourselves from every brother that walketh disorderly, and not after the tradition which he received of us.

PAUL WAS CHALLENGED WHEN the Thessalonians began to stray from the true doctrine of Christ that he taught them. The situation is grave today. It is clear that the world lives without the morality Jesus preached. It is hard to live among the unsaved and not become influenced by them.

It is likely that if you have suffered a period of estrangement from God during your Christian walk that bad company is to blame. It doesn't take much for a wedge to pry you away from things you know you should do and what you need. What you should do is obey God's word and what you need to do is love him and others, have trust in him, and remain in constant contact with him.

There are several interesting synonyms to describe disorderly: irregular, untidy, confused, unruly, chaotic, contrary, and immoral. Shunning all of those adjectives sounds like a hard job. It is true that following Jesus is not always easy. Did he not warn us of that? He said that the world may hate us but it hated him first (John 15:18).

Vigilance is necessary to protect the gifts we have through a close walk with him. Everywhere we go, the world is there. He commands us to turn our backs on their ways. Read in 2 Corinthians 6:17a, "Wherefore come out from among them, and be ye separate." Instead of allowing their ill and disorderly ways to jump onto your character, do the reverse. Let people see Christ in you and hope that they will be attracted to life, real and perpetual life.

I have been guilty of allowing evil communications to corrupt my good manners (1 Cor 15:33). The result was a lot of wasted time when instead of receiving my blessings as God's child I was exposed instead to his hand of chastening. Second Samuel 7:14 says, "I will be his father, and he shall be my son. If he commit iniquity, I will chasten him with the rod of men, and with the stripes of the children of men." The answer lies in forsaking those disorderly people who influence you. I do not mean to hate them but to turn from what they do and yes, if necessary—lead them out of your life. "As many as I love, I rebuke and chasten: be zealous therefore, and repent" (Rev 3:19).

Guard yourself. James reminds us to resist the devil and he will flee. Get to know people and decide how closely you should befriend them.

Week 39

Scripture text—Matthew 4:4

But he answered and said, It is written, Man shall not live
by bread alone, but by every word that proceedeth
out of the mouth of God.

JESUS MAKES IT CLEAR here that the Holy Bible is to be a part of our daily diet. Scripture is the Word of God sent to all people for nourishment. It says in 2 Timothy 3:16, "All scripture is given by inspiration of God, and is profitable for doctrine, for reproof, for correction, for instruction in righteousness."

Scoffers simply say that people wrote those words too but they don't follow through on the challenge given in John. In his Gospel he writes, "Search the scriptures; for in them ye think ye have eternal life: and they are they which testify of me" (5:39). Many people have come to know Christ through diligent study of the Bible. It teaches upon itself. "For precept must be upon precept, precept upon precept; line upon line, line upon line; here a little, and there a little" (Isa 28:10). To understand, study and cross reference.

A read through from Genesis to Revelation will likely do nothing but confuse the beginner. The curious may conclude that there are contradictions within. Read it again and again and again. If you have trouble with sections ask God for help and exercise faith. Books have been written to help. Here are some to look for: *Difficulties in the Bible* by Reuben A. Torrey and Edward D. Andrews, *Demolishing Supposed Bible Contradictions* by Ken Ham, *No Errors in my Bible, Sorry about Yours* by Mark Johansen, *When Critics Ask: A Popular Handbook on Bible Difficulties* by Norman L. Geisler.

Nothing makes me smile broader than when I learn about a Jewish person that has come to Christ after diligent Bible study. It cannot be denied, the Old Testament points to Christ. The books (Old and New Testaments) are of one accord concerning the past, present, and future plans of our Creator. I recommend that you spend day and night looking for the truth. You will find it. He is faithful. It is a happy lesson to know.

Read in Jeremiah 29:13, "And ye shall seek me, and find me, when ye shall search for me with all your heart." So along with your toast for breakfast, your sandwich for lunch, and your dumplings for dinner, open the Bible and find the best of what you need to live. John 10:10b says, "I am come that they might have life, and that they might have it more abundantly." Don't just exist, live.

In the end, it is up to us to learn about God. The Bible is full of exciting things. When I meet him face to face, I want him to know that I took an interest. I like bread but honestly scripture is more exciting. Paul reminds us that it is up to each individual. "Work out your own salvation with fear and trembling" (Phil 2:12b).

Week 40

Scripture text—Psalms 91:11-12

For he shall give his angels charge over thee, to keep thee in all thy ways. They shall bear thee up in their hands, lest thou dash thy foot against a stone.

CHRISTMAS WILL BE HERE soon and with it much talk about the angels of God. We know from reading Luke that it was Gabriel who God sent to give the blessed news about Jesus's coming divine birth to Mary. Imagine her fright. We also know from Matthew that the angel of the Lord appeared three times to Joseph to comfort and guide him concerning Jesus.

The angel of the Lord appeared to the shepherds in Bethlehem on the day of Jesus's birth to proclaim the Good News. Soon after, a whole multitude of angels appeared in celebration of the event (Luke 2:9-14). Angels are real and they are busy with tasks God gives them.

Michael, Gabriel, and Lucifer are mentioned by name in the King James Bible. So is Apollyon/Abaddon, the king of the locusts of the bottomless pit. We know what happens to the pompous Lucifer. Michael is the great archangel warrior and Gabriel seems to be a special messenger. He is surely of high rank although the term archangel is not directly associated with him in scripture.

God Likes Ants: Every Week

Angels worship God at his throne (Isa 6:3), they fight against Satan's fallen angels (Dan 10:13), they destroy evil at God's command (Gen 19:13), and they minister to the members of God's household (Heb 1:14). They take on the likeness of people at times. It says in Hebrews 13:2, "Be not forgetful to entertain strangers: for thereby some have entertained angels unawares."

They take a personal interest in us because God commands them to care for us and they are curious about us. Angels and humans are two different creations meant for different roles in God's blueprints. I suppose they wonder about us in much the same way that we wonder about them. They obey God in carrying our prayers, they protect us from evil, and like the feature scripture tells, they bear us into their hands to remove us from danger.

I have felt this physical protection many times. It is a comfort to know that the ministering spirits are close by ready at God's command to act on my behalf. It is a blessing that the people of the world do not know.

Satan himself quoted scripture to Jesus in Matthew 4:6 tempting him to call on the angels, "And saith unto him, If thou be the Son of God, cast thyself down: for it is written, He shall give his angels charge concerning thee: and in their hands they shall bear thee up, lest at any time thou dash thy foot against a stone." Jesus's answer was, "It is written again, Thou shall not tempt the Lord thy God" (4:7b). We must be vigilant as it is clear that Satan knows God's Word and likes to use it to confuse and entrap people.

Angels are servants of God just as people are intended to be. They must not be worshiped. Always throughout the Bible when a person bowed to an angel, the heavenly creature promptly corrected them. Paul said in Colossians 2:18a, "Let no man beguile you of your reward in a

Week 40

voluntary humility and worshipping of angels, intruding into those things which he hath not seen."

When you feel you may have been kept from danger by a thread or have felt the physical effects of angels in your life, thank God from whom the order of protection comes.

Week 41

Scripture text—Isaiah 9:6–7

For unto us a child is born, unto us a son is given: and the government shall be upon his shoulder: and his name shall be called Wonderful, Counselor, The mighty God, The everlasting Father, The Prince of Peace. Of the increase of his government and peace there shall be no end, upon the throne of David, and upon his kingdom, to order it, and to establish it with judgment and with justice from henceforth even forever. The zeal of the LORD of Hosts will perform this.

CHRISTMAS, THE SECOND MOST important day in Christianity, is here. It is sad that the people of the world do not recognize its true value. Resurrection Sunday is the bottom line for Christians but now we celebrate the Savior's birth.

This Old Testament passage declared the coming of Christ long before the day in Bethlehem that we celebrate this week. Jesus came to us as a tiny human. He existed eternally in Heaven but took on the flesh to endure all of human experience yet obeyed God perfectly. Something we cannot do and he knows it. His gift to us is himself and through knowing him we enjoy gifts immeasurable every day and onward through eternity. John 3:16 says, "For God so loved the world, that he gave his only begotten Son, that whosoever believeth in him should not perish, but have everlasting life."

Mary was blessed among women. She believed God when the angel told her as recorded in Luke 1:35, "And the angel answered and said unto her, The Holy Ghost shall come upon thee, and the power of the Highest shall overshadow thee: therefore also that holy thing which shall be called the Son of God." Only Jesus can claim this divinity as one with Father God. Consider the list of titles given to the Son above. He is called the Everlasting Father. He himself declares the truth. "I and my Father are one" (John 10:30).

He is our Savior. Luke chapter 2 gives us the Christmas story. We get the Good News, "For unto you is born this day in the city of David a Saviour, which is Christ the Lord" (2:11). He is all the things Isaiah said and his kingdom will be coming soon with perfect justice.

Christmas is about loving friends and family but much more about his loving us. Stop and remember each day what the word means—Christ-more. Make no apologies for loving him.

Week 42

Scripture text—2 Timothy 2:23

But foolish and unlearned questions avoid, knowing that they do gender strifes.

MANY OF OUR CONVERSATIONS today are carried on without thought or consideration. We ask and answer questions before we even know what we want to say. Words are powerful. The truest example of this is scripture itself. We should examine the words we use before letting them slide past our lips.

Foolish means ill considered, lacking forethought, resulting from a lack of sense, and ignorant. Unlearned means not known through study or instruction. Gender when used as it is here is an obsolete (to me) use of the word meaning to breed. The result equals strife: bitter conflict, discord, antagonism, quarrel, competition, and rivalry.

I define the words above because such as we often speak without thought, sometimes we read without understanding. Listening to sentences can help us learn to speak with clarity and purpose. It is most often best to be quiet but if you must speak, make the words count for good.

Learning to think before you speak takes practice (even faith) but the result is a more tranquil existence and

Week 42

relationship with others. In Romans 14:19 Paul gives good advice. "Let us therefore follow after the things which make for peace, and things wherewith one may edify another."

If you don't know what you are talking about, don't talk. If you are emotional and can't say something nice, don't talk. If it is gossip, don't talk. If someone speaks harmfully to you and it's not fair, don't talk.

Don't boast. "He is proud, knowing nothing, but doting about questions and strifes of words, whereof cometh envy, strife, railings, evil surmising" (1 Tim 6:4). If you want to communicate with other people using words than make choices that edify, enlighten, improve, and educate. Be certain of what you want to say and then make it a goal to bring good results in the discourse.

One of my favorite verses is Ecclesiastes 5:2. Try to memorize it. "Be not rash with thy mouth, and let not thine heart be hasty to utter anything before God: for God is in heaven, and thou upon earth: therefore let thy words be few." Remembering that God hears all will keep us from forgetting our role which is to love our neighbor as ourselves. Practice indeed.

Week 43

Scripture text—Matthew 10:34

Think not that I am come to send peace on earth:
I came not to send peace, but a sword.

Peace sounds wonderful but it cannot be the bottom line. Devotion to Jesus Christ must be the ultimate factor in our lives. The Prince of Peace will rule over this planet in righteousness and justice but not until he comes to usher in his kingdom. All humans are sinners and our best efforts fall short (Rom 3:23). We cannot attain peace without direct intervention from above.

It is inevitable that there will be battles between the truth and the lies put forth by Satan, who is the current prince of this planet. He is the spirit that works in the children of disobedience (Eph 2:2). For now, the Holy Spirit that indwells believers is the force of light in a dark world.

Wars have been waged down through the ages in the name of God and religion. I might proffer that those that thought they were on the right side may not have been. Jesus spoke out against religion and its trappings. Often religious leaders are vessels for the enemy.

What Jesus meant in the above verse is that as his followers, we can expect bitter derision even to the point of *swords* with those close to us that are not in the household of God. The chapter continues, "For I am come to set a man at variance against his father; and the daughter against her mother, and the daughter in law against her mother in law. And a man's foes shall be they of his own household. He that loveth father or mother more than me is not worthy of me: and he that loveth son or daughter more than me is not worthy of me" (35–37).

Surround yourself with other Christians for the sake of edifying, fellowship, and accountability. It will increase the chances of peaceful living. Our family, however, is our family regardless of conflicting world views. Expect to defend your faith and forsake them for Christ if need be.

The war of wars is yet to come. The culmination of our age will end with the bloodiest war yet fought. Revelation 16:16 says, "And he gathered them together into a place called in the Hebrew tongue Armageddon." Christ will finally destroy [that Wicked] with the brightness of his coming (2 Thess 2:8). Study prophesies—it won't be long now.

It is a real war between good and evil. God wins. Remain on the winning side and pray. Pray for those lost in the world and pray in thanksgiving to the Lord who holds you safely in his right hand.

Week 44

Scripture text—Matthew 18:21-22

Then came Peter to him, and said, Lord, how oft shall my brother sin against me, and I forgive him? till seven times? Jesus saith unto him, I say not unto thee, Until seven times: but Until seventy times seven.

Peter was more generous than most with his choice of seven as the number of times one might forgive another's trespass. The three chances rule comes to my mind. Three strikes and you are out. God does not like my idea or Peter's. Jesus clearly shows how God's ways are not our ways and how much higher his ways are than our ways (Isa 55:9).

Seventy times seven means 490 times. I believe he meant as many times as is necessary or basically every time. This means humbling yourself and realizing that holding onto grudges creates more harm than it is worth for both parties. Not to mention, it is told us in Matthew 6:14, "For if ye forgive men their trespasses, your heavenly Father will also forgive you." I love God's promises. He is reliable and faithful.

Pride, the prolonging of strife, and wasting of mental energy are some results of failing to forgive others. While forgiveness is not independently listed as a fruit of the Spirit

Week 44

in Galatians chapter 5, it would be in fair company to the nine that are. God gives the fruit of the Spirit against which there is no law: love, joy, peace, longsuffering, gentleness, goodness, faith, meekness, and temperance (Gal 5:22–23).

Don't harbor hatred and fear, or place blame. Trust in God to look out for your interests. Paul reminds us of God's plan in Romans 12:19, "Dearly beloved, avenge not yourselves, but rather give place unto wrath: for it is written, Vengeance is mine; I will repay, saith the Lord."

If someone has wronged you, keep the big picture in mind and run for the prize, heavenly peace and rest.

Week 45

Scripture text—James 5:16

Confess your faults one to another, and pray one for another, that ye may be healed. The effectual fervent prayer of a righteous man availeth much.

WHEN WE FEEL DISTANT from our Lord because of guilt that is just the time to get with another Christian and talk about it. We must support one another without judgment. "Judge not, that ye be not judged" (Matt 7:1). Remember we all struggle with something. Let us make it a priority to bear one another's burdens and share in petitioning God.

In our natural state we are not righteous. Not a single person is righteous on his/her own merit (Rom 3:12, Pss 14:3, 53:3). It is through faith in Christ Jesus that we are made perfectly righteous, clean, and are able to approach God's throne boldly. Admit your need for him because you are a sinner and receive the gift of effectual prayer. Faith justifies (Rom 4:5). In Hebrews, many examples are given of Old Testament saints that were justified through faith. Jesus had yet to be born in Bethlehem in their day but he is eternal.

The verse states that confessing faults and praying for others combine in the process of healing. Share your faults

Week 45

and weaknesses. Ask others for prayer and pray for them. The intense, zealous prayer of a person justified through Christ is heard and answered.

Memorized repetitious prayers without substance are not fervent prayers (Matt 6:7). Pour out all of your thoughts, fears, hopes, doubts, desires, frustrations, disappointments, praises, gratitude, and dreams to the Creator of the universe who is more than capable of caring for you. These types of fervent prayers get results as promised above.

God will always answer the prayers of the righteous. Let him answer in his wisdom and in his time. This is hard. Practice resting in his perfect peace while you wait. Trust him. Psalms 55:17 promises, "Evening, and morning, and at noon, will I pray, and cry aloud: and he shall hear my voice."

Week 46

Scripture text—Mark 10:27

And Jesus looking upon them saith, With men it is impossible, but not with God: for with God all things are possible.

Even as a Christian, I find myself worrying sometimes about the hows of my life. I wonder: How can I do that? there are too many obstacles in my path. How can I wait another minute for God to take action on my behalf?

Living with the human time schedule and in limited understanding, I often fail at faith. It is a good thing that he is the Comforter. The main thing is to talk to him about all of it: doubts, fears, and failings. We know that he is faithful and true (Rev 19:11). We know he is aware of our circumstances and knows what we need before we ask him (Matt 6:8). We know he created the universe with the power of his Word (Gen 1). Let us also know that he loves us more than we can imagine and that he knows we struggle with these feelings of doubt and fear.

He knows our frailties and that our lives are naught without him. Psalms 103:14 says, "For he knoweth our frame; he remembereth that we are dust." God's mercies are fresh every morning (Lam 3:22–23). All things are possible with God.

Week 46

He can change, rearrange, remove, or guide you through those obstacles. He gives peace that passes understanding while we are waiting for his actions. If we are feeling sad and impatient about our circumstances or about the state of our faith, remember God will never fail or forsake his children.

Focus on him. The things that cloud our faith get pushed aside by his love and permanent presence by our side and in our hearts. Ask him like the man in Mark 9:24 did, "And straightway the father of the child cried out, and said with tears, Lord, I believe; help thou mine unbelief."

Week 47

Scripture text—2 Corinthians 4:8-9

We are troubled on every side, yet not distressed; we are perplexed, but not in despair; Persecuted, but not forsaken; cast down, but not destroyed.

THE LETTER OF PAUL'S was addressed to the church. We as Christians can expect to experience the first situation in each clause but that the Lord will surely protect us from the second more devastating action. In our walk with Christ, we will be troubled, perplexed, persecuted, and cast down.

Even with God's fresh mercies, in a sinful world and living with the flesh, they are sure. The good news is that Jesus walks with us and keeps us from harm and provides comfort and direction. First Corinthians 10:13 tells us, "There hath no temptation taken you but such as is common to man: But God is faithful, who will not suffer you to be tempted above that ye are able; but will with the temptation also make a way to escape, that ye may be able to bear it."

At times we argue with God that we are not able to bear it, but praise God, he knows us and our capabilities much better than we ourselves do. This is where our faith is practiced. And it does take practice and experience knowing Christ to trust that he is faithful and our faith in him

Week 47

is not in vain. So let us rejoice in hope, have patience in tribulation, and continue in prayer (Rom 12:12).

Trust him to see you through your trials. Talk to him and open yourself up to his peace and grace. Philippians 4:6 reminds us that worry is not necessary with a God that knows us. Prayer is vital. "Be careful [anxious] for nothing; but in everything by prayer and supplication with thanksgiving let your requests be made known to God."

We will not suffer distress (great pain, anxiety, sorrow) and despair (loss of hope). We will not be forsaken (abandoned) nor destroyed (defeated). If you feel like you are, reassess yourself and accept God's promise.

Week 48

Scripture text—Psalms 122:6

Pray for the peace of Jerusalem:
they shall prosper that love thee.

ISRAEL AND JERUSALEM WILL survive. The headlines in the world news have been very disturbing but we must remember that all the threats to Israel's existence are fantasy. God holds Israel as the apple of his eye (Deut 32:10). He will intervene on their behalf. It is impossible not to follow along in the Bible with the events happening in our current newscasts. We know from prophecy that the only peace to come to the region will be God's kingdom. It will be a hard, bloody road until then. That is clear.

Jerusalem will be the center of all things. It is the chosen city like Israel is the chosen people. Any true Christian is adopted into the chosen family through faith. Like Abraham, Sarah, and Noah believed God and were justified by faith (Heb 11), so are we.

First Kings 11:36 tells of the chosen city, "And unto his son will I give one tribe, that David my servant may have a light alway before me in Jerusalem, the city which I have chosen me to put my name there." It would not take much to obliterate the tiny nation of God's own people. Pray for

Week 48

Israel. It will please the Lord. America must support Israel in order to maintain the blessings and prosperity God has given.

Pray for the leadership of Israel who has to face impossible decisions imminently. Pray for the leaders of the world's nations. They will be judged according to their relationship to Israel, see Matthew chapter 25. He is serious when he said in Genesis 12:3a, "And I will bless them that bless thee, and curse him that curseth thee."

Prayer points are endless. Not only are the nations in the Middle East affecting Israel and America, but Russia, China and Europe. All has been prophesied in scripture. So many people are caught up in the cares of their lives that the things that really concern us all go ignored. Thank goodness for those who pay attention and look upwards. And for the rest, open your Bible and turn on the news.

"It is a fearful thing to fall into the hands of the living God" (Heb 10:31).

Week 49

Scripture text—Proverbs 12:16

A fool's wrath is presently known: but a prudent man covereth shame.

As I read through Proverbs this morning, this verse caught my attention and brought to mind the incredible things that people post on the modern phenomenon of social media. This past Sunday, my pastor challenged us to think about what makes us blush in today's world. We have become desensitized to evil since it is so rampant.

I get embarrassed for people that use sick language and purposefully hurt others in the friend forum. Some things are just better kept private. What is worse is when people think it is funny and share the shameful exchanges.

It is an example of people's loss of self-control. Certainly there are instances in our days when we get angry, feel slighted, or are mistreated. Emotion surfaces. Practice discretion before responding. Discretion is using common sense, having wisdom, and making responsible decisions. Proverbs 19:11 says, "The discretion of a man deferreth his anger; and it is his glory to pass over a transgression." Let the Lord handle your battles. Pray for his peace to keep you from lashing out.

We may shudder when faced with social media posts, headlines, and conversations we hear during our day. As Christians, let's work hard to follow Paul's advice in Ephesians. "Let no corrupt communication proceed out of your mouth [or our fingertips on a keyboard], but that which is good to the use of edifying, that it may minister grace to the hearers" (4:29).

My wonderful pastor told a story of a man that kept a stone in his mouth and had to remove it to speak an answer to others. This is a great idea but could cause tooth damage. It is impractical but the idea is smart. If we could only think for a bit before responding to words and actions we will keep our dignity intact and offer grace to the people who hurt us.

Proverbs 2:11 says, "Discretion shall preserve thee, understanding shall keep thee." Get in the habit of placing all things into God's capable hands. He will manage all of your affairs for the best.

Week 50

Scripture text—Zechariah 14:12

And this shall be the plague wherewith the LORD will smite all the people that have fought against Jerusalem; Their flesh shall consume away while they stand upon their feet, and their eyes shall consume away in their holes, and their tongue shall consume away in their mouth.

THE PROPHETIC BOOK OF Zechariah does not mince words about the fate of Israel's enemies. It is hard not to focus on this topic with the headlines in the news daily telling of the escalating disputes in the Middle East.

We know the day will come when the things described by Zechariah will come to pass. It will be horrific. Soon after, Jesus will set up his kingdom right here on earth. Isaiah 32:1 says, "Behold a king shall rule in righteousness, and princes shall rule in judgment." The Lord will be king over the whole earth (Zech 14:9). It is hard to keep one's mind on daily human trouble when this truth of the future is so near. It is a good thing to consider God's plans instead of our tiny worries.

The words in the feature verse sound like the result of nuclear war, do they not? A fiery future awaits the earth and destruction to those who oppose Israel. God will save his

Week 50

people out from this fire. These people include Israel and those who have been adopted into God's family through faith in the Lord (Eph 1:5).

Israel's enemies may seek her destruction through nuclear means but God will turn that around onto their own heads with the brightness of his coming. Paul said in 2 Thessalonians 2:8, "And then shall that Wicked be revealed, whom the Lord shall consume with the spirit of his mouth, and shall destroy with the brightness of his coming."

What can each of us do to be ready? Most importantly, accept God's gift of salvation through faith in Christ. Study the prophetic books of the Bible and pay attention to the world news. Pray for Israel.

After the Time of Jacob's Trouble (the tribulation), Jesus will be the king on the earth ruling Jerusalem from the throne of David. What a wonderful time it will be, be sure and be there.

Week 51

Scripture text—Proverbs 24:17-18

Rejoice not when thine enemy falleth, and let not thine heart be glad when he stumbleth: Lest the LORD see it, and it displease him, and he turn away his wrath from him.

THESE VERSES ARE MEANT to check our attitude during our daily lives. There are people that take advantage of us, lie to us, purposefully throw stumbling blocks in our path, get the promotion we expected, and more serious matters (murder our family member, burn down our house).

We cannot change other people's behavior. We can only check our hearts and minds when these types of things happen to us. Harboring gladness in our heart when the person who hurts or mistreats us *gets what's coming to them* shows faithlessness. God promises to handle our battles for us.

If you have been truly wronged, let go and let God. This phrase is used a lot in today's world, but is a valuable technique when we find ourselves seeking someone's hurt. Deuteronomy 32:35 says, "To me [God] belongeth vengeance, and recompence; their foot shall slide in due time: for the day of their calamity is at hand, and the things that shall come upon them make haste."

Week 51

God searches our hearts and is displeased when we do not love others as ourselves. That is the heart of God's expectation of us (Gal 5:13). Have we done wrong to others? Certainly we have. Only God knows all circumstances and can bring the bad things in life around for good, "But as for you, ye thought evil against me; but God meant it unto good, to bring to pass, as it is this day, to save much people alive" (Gen 50:20).

God is sovereign. He can turn our ill thoughts toward our enemies into a blessing for them and back fire on us. He gets his way so why not do it his way first. Bring every thought into subjection to the Lord (2 Cor 10:5). Let us give people a break. It shows discretion and glory to pass over matters that we think should be avenged (Prov 19:11). God is more equipped to decide and act.

Patience takes practice and there are times when it will not be possible to see eye to eye with others. We must; however, forgive people and give our all to living peacefully with everyone. All God asks is our best effort and then he will take care of the rest (Rom 12:18). When we feel overpowered with emotion because our enemies seem too strong for us, remember they are not. God is our deliverer (2 Sam 22:18).

If you want things to go well with you, do not wish ill upon anyone. Instead as Matthew 5:44 says, "But I say unto you, Love your enemies, bless them that curse you, do good to them that hate you, and pray for them which despitefully use you, and persecute you."

As usual, prayer is the answer. Acts 8:22 stresses this, "Repent therefore of this thy wickedness, and pray God, if perhaps the thought of thine heart may be forgiven thee."

Week 52

Scripture text—1 Timothy 1:17

Now unto the King eternal, immortal, invisible, the only wise God, be honour and glory for ever and ever, Amen.

I FEEL BLESSED THAT my God has given me the eyes to recognize him. The adjectives above only scratch the surface of the titles he holds and hint at the praise that he deserves. Many people today say they do not worship God because he must be a narcissist or egomaniac to expect reverence and praise. How sad, they either forget or do not know who he is. To me, the folks that say those things are the ones with the ego trouble.

We who are on earth must remember who is in Heaven (Eccl 5:2) and how far above our ways are his ways (Isa 55:9). It is because he is eternal, immortal, invisible, and wise that we wake up each day with the ability to draw a breath. What a pity that the people in the world cannot see the gifts freely given to them even as unbelievers. The gifts to believers are beyond imagination, my favorite being free access to the throne room.

First Chronicles 16:29 says, "Give unto the LORD the glory due unto his name: bring an offering, and come before him: worship the LORD in the beauty of holiness."

Week 52

The gifts I enjoy from the Lord are wonderful. Everything comes from him: soap, feather pillows, clean water, my dad, hot running water, the first spring flower on the bush by my porch, literacy, toothpaste, and everything else. The Bible tells me to give him worship and glory because he exists. He is certainly worthy of the praise of our tongues continuously.

He is the past, present, and future. Happy will I be to enter into glory donning a new sparkling incorruptible and immortal body as he has promised (1 Cor 15:53). For now, I am in the flesh walking about on his footstool. The earth is described as God's footstool many times in scripture. I hope to please him with as much appreciation as his holiness can hear, "Exalt ye the LORD our God, and worship at his footstool; for he is holy" (Ps 99:5). Join me won't you.

Appendix A

What I believe

I believe God is One represented in three persons: God the Father, God the Son (Jesus Christ—The Word), and God the Holy Spirit.

I believe Jesus Christ is eternal and was present in Heaven before his incarnation as a human being born of the Virgin Mary through direct intervention of The Holy Spirit.

I believe Jesus's death was orchestrated by God to bring salvation to all people. Every individual deserves death as punishment for sin. God himself took the place of each person as a cleansing substitute, paying in his blood. Salvation is based on believe in this truth through faith.

I believe in the resurrection of Jesus Christ and eventually the resurrection of all people for individual judgment.

I believe the Bible is God's infallible and inspired Word.

I believe in a literal Heaven and a literal Hell.

www.ingramcontent.com/pod-product-compliance
Lightning Source LLC
Chambersburg PA
CBHW070457090426
42735CB00012B/2591